W9-CHN-886

GOD'S PROMISES for the GOLDEN YEARS

GOD'S PROMISES for the GOLDEN YEARS

WORD PUBLISHING
Dallas • London • Vancouver • Melbourne

GOD'S PROMISES FOR THE GOLDEN YEARS

Unless otherwise noted, Scripture quotations are from *The Holy Bible, King James Version*.

Library of Congress Cataloging-in-Publication Data

God's promises for the golden years.
p. cm.
ISBN 0-8499-5170-4 (bonded leather)
1. Aging—Prayer-books and devotions—English. 2. God—Promises-Prayer Books and devotions— I. Word Publishing.
BV4580.G63 1995
242'.65—dc20 95-18129
CIP

Printed in Belgium

Contents

When Troubles Come And You're Sick...

God Promises Healing

To the chief Musician on Neginoth upon Sheminith, A Psalm of David. O LORD, rebuke me not in thine anger, neither chasten me in thy hot displeasure.

Have mercy upon me, O LORD; for I am weak: O LORD, heal me; for my bones are vexed.

Psalms 6:1, 2

...If thou wilt diligently hearken to the voice of the LORD thy God, and wilt do that which is right in his sight, and wilt give ear to his commandments, and keep all his statutes, I will put none of these diseases upon thee, which I have brought upon the Egyptians: for I am the LORD that healeth thee.

Exodus 15:26

O LORD my God, I cried unto thee, and thou hast healed me.

O LORD, thou hast brought up my soul from the grave: thou hast kept me alive, that I should not go down to the pit.

Sing unto the LORD, O ye saints of his, and give thanks at the remembrance of his holiness.

Psalms 30:2-4

Then they cry unto the LORD in their trouble, and he saveth them out of their distresses.

He sent his word, and healed them, and delivered them from their destructions.

Psalms 107:19, 20

Heal me, O LORD, and I shall be healed; save me, and I shall be saved: for thou art my praise.

Jeremiah 17:14

Is any sick among you? let him call for the elders of the church; and let them pray over him, anointing him with oil in the name of the Lord:

And the prayer of faith shall save the sick, and the Lord shall raise him up; and if he have committed sins, they shall be forgiven him.

James 5:14, 15

God Is With You

To the chief Musician on Neginoth, A Psalm or Song. God be merciful unto us, and bless us; and cause his face to shine upon us; Selah.

That thy way may be known upon earth, thy saving health among all nations.

Let the people praise thee, O God; let all the people praise thee.

Psalms 67:1-3

Why art thou cast down, O my soul? and why art thou disquieted within me? hope thou in God: for I shall yet praise him, who is the health of my countenance, and my God.

Psalms 42:11

In the fear of the LORD is strong confidence: and his children shall have a place of refuge.

The fear of the LORD is a fountain of life, to depart from the snares of death.

Proverbs 14:26, 27

In the day of my trouble I sought the Lord: my sore ran in the night, and ceased not: my soul refused to be comforted.

I remembered God, and was troubled: I complained, and my spirit was overwhelmed. Selah.

Thou holdest mine eyes waking: I am so troubled that I cannot speak.

I have considered the days of old, the years of ancient times.

I call to remembrance my song in the night: I commune with mine own heart: and my spirit made diligent search.

Will the Lord cast off for ever? and will he be favourable no more?

Is his mercy clean gone for ever? doth his promise fail for evermore?

Hath God forgotten to be gracious? hath he in anger shut up his tender mercies? Selah.

And I said, This is my infirmity: but I will remember the years of the right hand of the most High.

Psalms 77:2-10

In the day of my trouble I will call upon thee: for thou wilt answer me.

Psalms 86:7

I can do all things through Christ which strengtheneth me.

Philippians 4:13

God Gives You Hope

To the chief Musician on Neginoth, A Psalm of David. Hear me when I call, O God of my righteousness: thou hast enlarged me when I was in distress; have mercy upon me, and hear my prayer.

Psalms 4:1

To the chief Musician, A Psalm of David. I waited patiently for the LORD; and he inclined unto me, and heard my cry.

And he hath put a new song in my mouth, even praise unto our God: many shall see it, and fear, and shall trust in the LORD.

Psalms 40:1, 3

O give thanks unto the LORD, for he is good: for his mercy endureth for ever.

Let the redeemed of the LORD say so, whom he hath redeemed from the hand of the enemy;

And gathered them out of the lands, from the east, and from the west, from the north, and from the south.

They wandered in the wilderness in a solitary way; they found no city to dwell in.

Hungry and thirsty, their soul fainted in them.

Then they cried unto the LORD in their trouble, and he delivered them out of their distresses.

Psalms 107:1-6

Be careful for nothing; but in every thing by prayer and supplication with thanksgiving let your requests be made known unto God.

And the peace of God, which passeth all understanding, shall keep your hearts and minds through Christ Jesus.

Philippians 4:6, 7

And Jesus said unto the centurion, Go thy way; and as thou hast believed, so be it done unto thee. And his servant was healed in the selfsame hour.

And when Jesus was come into Peter's house, he saw his wife's mother laid, and sick of a fever.

And he touched her hand, and the fever left her: and she arose, and ministered unto them.

When the even was come, they brought unto him many that were possessed with devils: and he cast out the spirits with his word, and healed all that were sick:

That it might be fulfilled which was spoken by Esaias the prophet, saying, Himself took our infirmities, and bare our sicknesses.

Matthew 8:13-17

And I said, My strength and my hope is perished from the LORD:

Remembering mine affliction and my misery, the wormwood and the gall.

My soul hath them still in remembrance, and is humbled in me.

This I recall to my mind, therefore have I hope.

It is of the LORD'S mercies that we are not consumed, because his compassions fail not.

They are new every morning: great is thy faithfulness.

The LORD is my portion, saith my soul; therefore will I hope in him.

Lamentations 3:18-24

When Troubles Come And You're Worried About Finances…

God Promises To Meet Your Needs

The LORD redeemeth the soul of his servants: and none of them that trust in him shall be desolate.

Psalms 34:22

The young lions do lack, and suffer hunger: but they that seek the LORD shall not want any good thing.

Psalms 34:10

He found him in a desert land, and in the waste howling wilderness; he led him about, he instructed him, he kept him as the apple of his eye.

As an eagle stirreth up her nest, fluttereth over her young, spreadeth abroad her wings, taketh them, beareth them on her wings:

So the LORD alone did lead him, and there was no strange god with him.

He made him ride on the high places of the earth, that he might eat the increase of the fields; and he made him to suck honey out of the rock, and oil out of the flinty rock;

Deuteronomy 32:10-13

Trust in the LORD, and do good; so shalt thou dwell in the land, and verily thou shalt be fed.

Psalms 37:3

When the poor and needy seek water, and there is none, and their tongue faileth for thirst, I the LORD will hear them, I the God of Israel will not forsake them.

Isaiah 41:17

The people asked, and he brought quails, and satisfied them with the bread of heaven.

Psalms 105:40

Who is like unto the LORD our God, who dwelleth on high,

Who humbleth himself to behold the things that are in heaven, and in the earth!

He raiseth up the poor out of the dust, and lifteth the needy out of the dunghill;

Psalms 113:5-7

Then shalt thou call, and the LORD shall answer; thou shalt cry, and he shall say, Here I am. If thou take away from the midst of thee the yoke, the putting forth of the finger, and speaking vanity;

And if thou draw out thy soul to the hungry, and satisfy the afflicted soul; then shall thy light rise in obscurity, and thy darkness be as the noon day:

And the LORD shall guide thee continually, and satisfy thy soul in drought, and make fat thy bones: and thou shalt be like a watered garden, and like a spring of water, whose waters fail not.

Isaiah 58:9-11

Therefore I say unto you, Take no thought for your life, what ye shall eat, or what ye shall drink; nor yet for your body, what ye shall put on. Is not the life more than meat, and the body than raiment?

Behold the fowls of the air: for they sow not, neither do they reap, nor gather into barns; yet your heavenly Father feedeth them. Are ye not much better than they?

Which of you by taking thought can add one cubit unto his stature?

And why take ye thought for raiment? Consider the lilies of the field, how they grow; they toil not, neither do they spin:

And yet I say unto you, That even Solomon in all his glory was not arrayed like one of these.

Matthew 6:25-29

How excellent is thy lovingkindness, O God! therefore the children of men put their trust under the shadow of thy wings.

They shall be abundantly satisfied with the fatness of thy house; and thou shalt make them drink of the river of thy pleasures.

For with thee is the fountain of life: in thy light shall we see light.

O continue thy lovingkindness unto them that know thee; and thy righteousness to the upright in heart.

Psalms 36:7-10

God Blesses You With His Wealth

A Psalm of David. The earth is the LORD'S, and the fulness thereof; the world, and they that dwell therein.

Psalms 24:1

Ask of me, and I shall give thee the heathen for thine inheritance, and the uttermost parts of the earth for thy possession.

Psalms 2:8

Thou visitest the earth, and waterest it: thou greatly enrichest it with the river of God, which is full of water: thou preparest them corn, when thou hast so provided for it.

Thou waterest the ridges thereof abundantly: thou settlest the furrows thereof: thou makest it soft with showers: thou blessest the springing thereof.

Thou crownest the year with thy goodness; and thy paths drop fatness.

Psalms 65:9-11

If they obey and serve him, they shall spend their days in prosperity, and their years in pleasures.

Job 36:11

He hath filled the hungry with good things; and the rich he hath sent empty away.

Luke 1:53

O bless our God, ye people, and make the voice of his praise to be heard:

Which holdeth our soul in life, and suffereth not our feet to be moved.

For thou, O God, hast proved us: thou hast tried us, as silver is tried.

Thou broughtest us into the net; thou laidst affliction upon our loins.

Thou hast caused men to ride over our heads; we went through fire and through water: but thou broughtest us out into a wealthy place.

Psalms 66:8-12

For the LORD is a great God, and a great King above all gods.

In his hand are the deep places of the earth: the strength of the hills is his also.

The sea is his, and he made it: and his hands formed the dry land.

O come, let us worship and bow down: let us kneel before the LORD our maker.

For he is our God; and we are the people of his pasture, and the sheep of his hand.

Psalms 95:3-7

God Says He'll Be With You Even If You're Poor

Behold, God is mighty, and despiseth not any: he is mighty in strength and wisdom.

He preserveth not the life of the wicked: but giveth right to the poor.

Job 36:5, 6

But I am poor and needy: make haste unto me, O God: thou art my help and my deliverer; O LORD, make no tarrying.

Psalms 70:5

But he saveth the poor from the sword, from their mouth, and from the hand of the mighty.

So the poor hath hope, and iniquity stoppeth her mouth.

Job 5:15, 16

A little that a righteous man hath is better than the riches of many wicked.

For the arms of the wicked shall be broken: but the LORD upholdeth the righteous.

The LORD knoweth the days of the upright: and their inheritance shall be for ever.

They shall not be ashamed in the evil time: and in the days of famine they shall be satisfied.

Psalms 37:16-19

Consider the ravens: for they neither sow nor reap; which neither have storehouse nor barn; and God feedeth them: how much more are ye better than the fowls?

And which of you with taking thought can add to his stature one cubit?

If ye then be not able to do that thing which is least, why take ye thought for the rest?

Consider the lilies how they grow: they toil not, they spin not; and yet I say unto you, that Solomon in all his glory was not arrayed like one of these.

If then God so clothe the grass, which is to day in the field, and to morrow is cast into the oven; how much more will he clothe you, O ye of little faith?

Luke 12:24-28

I know both how to be abased, and I know how to abound: every where and in all things I am instructed both to be full and to be hungry, both to abound and to suffer need.

I can do all things through Christ which strengtheneth me.

Philippians 4:12, 13

I will be glad and rejoice in thy mercy: for thou hast considered my trouble; thou hast known my soul in adversities;

Psalms 31:7

When Troubles Come And Your Children Don't Call…

God Comforts You

Comfort ye, comfort ye my people, saith your God.

Isaiah 40:1

A Psalm of David. Unto thee will I cry, O LORD my rock; be not silent to me: lest, if thou be silent to me, I become like them that go down into the pit.

Hear the voice of my supplications, when I cry unto thee, when I lift up my hands toward thy holy oracle.

Psalms 28:1, 2

He shall feed his flock like a shepherd: he shall gather the lambs with his arm, and carry them in his bosom, and shall gently lead those that are with young.

Isaiah 40:11

And the son said unto him, Father, I have sinned against heaven, and in thy sight, and am no more worthy to be called thy son.

But the father said to his servants, Bring forth the best robe, and put it on him; and put a ring on his hand, and shoes on his feet:

And bring hither the fatted calf, and kill it; and let us eat, and be merry:

For this my son was dead, and is alive again; he was lost, and is found. And they began to be merry.

Luke 15:21-24

Yea, though I walk through the valley of the shadow of death, I will fear no evil: for thou art with me; thy rod and thy staff they comfort me.

Psalms 23:4

For whatsoever things were written aforetime were written for our learning, that we through patience and comfort of the scriptures might have hope.

Romans 15:4

God Tells You How To Love Them

If a son shall ask bread of any of you that is a father, will he give him a stone? or if he ask a fish, will he for a fish give him a serpent?

Or if he shall ask an egg, will he offer him a scorpion?

If ye then, being evil, know how to give good gifts unto your children: how much more shall your heavenly Father give the Holy Spirit to them that ask him?

Luke 11:11-13

Be ye therefore merciful, as your Father also is merciful.

Judge not, and ye shall not be judged: condemn not, and ye shall not be condemned: forgive, and ye shall be forgiven:

Give, and it shall be given unto you; good measure, pressed down, and shaken together, and running over, shall men give into your bosom. For with the same measure that ye mete withal it shall be measured to you again.

Luke 6:36-38

Hatred stirreth up strifes: but love covereth all sins.

Proverbs 10:12

And he said, A certain man had two sons:

And the younger of them said to his father, Father, give me the portion of goods that falleth to me. And he divided unto them his living.

And not many days after the younger son gathered all together, and took his journey into a far country, and there wasted his substance with riotous living.

And when he had spent all, there arose a mighty famine in that land; and he began to be in want.

And he went and joined himself to a citizen of that country; and he sent him into his fields to feed swine.

And he would fain have filled his belly with the husks that the swine did eat: and no man gave unto him.

And when he came to himself, he said, How many hired servants of my father's have bread enough and to spare, and I perish with hunger!

I will arise and go to my father, and will say unto him, Father, I have sinned against heaven, and before thee,

And am no more worthy to be called thy son: make me as one of thy hired servants.

And he arose, and came to his father. But when he was yet a great way off, his father saw him, and had compassion, and ran, and fell on his neck, and kissed him.

Luke 15:11-20

A friend loveth at all times, and a brother is born for adversity.

Proverbs 17:17

Charity suffereth long, and is kind; charity envieth not; charity vaunteth not itself, is not puffed up,

Doth not behave itself unseemly, seeketh not her own, is not easily provoked, thinketh no evil;

Rejoiceth not in iniquity, but rejoiceth in the truth;

Beareth all things, believeth all things, hopeth all things, endureth all things.

I Corinthians 13:4-7

God Promises They'll Grow As You've Taught Them

The just man walketh in his integrity: his children are blessed after him.

Proverbs 20:7

Gather the people together, men, and women, and children, and thy stranger that is within thy gates, that they may hear, and that they may learn, and fear the LORD your God, and observe to do all the words of this law:

And that their children, which have not known any thing, may hear, and learn to fear the LORD your God, as long as ye live in the land whither ye go over Jordan to possess it.

Deuteronomy 31:12, 13

Now therefore write ye this song for you, and teach it the children of Israel: put it in their mouths, that this song may be a witness for me against the children of Israel.

For when I shall have brought them into the land which I sware unto their fathers, that floweth with milk and honey; and they shall have eaten and filled themselves, and waxen fat; then will they turn unto other gods, and serve them, and provoke me, and break my covenant.

And it shall come to pass, when many evils and troubles are befallen them, that this song shall testify against them as a witness; for it shall not be forgotten out of the mouths of their seed: for I know their imagination which they go about, even now, before I have brought them into the land which I sware.

Deuteronomy 31:19-21

Therefore shall ye lay up these my words in your heart and in your soul, and bind them for a sign upon your hand, that they may be as frontlets between your eyes.

And ye shall teach them your children, speaking of them when thou sittest in thine house, and when thou walkest by the way, when thou liest down, and when thou risest up.

And thou shalt write them upon the door posts of thine house, and upon thy gates:

That your days may be multiplied, and the days of your children, in the land which the LORD sware unto your fathers to give them, as the days of heaven upon the earth.

Deuteronomy 11:18-21

When I call to remembrance the unfeigned faith that is in thee, which dwelt first in thy grandmother Lois, and thy mother Eunice; and I am persuaded that in thee also.

II Timothy 1:5

And his mercy is on them that fear him from generation to generation.

Luke 1:50

When Troubles Come And Your Friends Leave You…

God Remains At Your Side

As one whom his mother comforteth, so will I comfort you; and ye shall be comforted in Jerusalem.

Isaiah 66:13

My friends scorn me: but mine eye poureth out tears unto God.

Job 16:20

To the chief Musician on Neginoth, Maschil, A Psalm of David, when the Ziphims came and said to Saul, Doth not David hide himself with us? Save me, O God, by thy name, and judge me by thy strength.

Hear my prayer, O God; give ear to the words of my mouth.

For strangers are risen up against me, and oppressors seek after my soul: they have not set God before them. Selah.

Behold, God is mine helper: the Lord is with them that uphold my soul.

Psalms 54:1-4

The troubles of my heart are enlarged: O bring thou me out of my distresses.

Look upon mine affliction and my pain; and forgive all my sins.

Consider mine enemies; for they are many; and they hate me with cruel hatred.

O keep my soul, and deliver me: let me not be ashamed; for I put my trust in thee.

Let integrity and uprightness preserve me; for I wait on thee.

Redeem Israel, O God, out of all his troubles.

Psalms 25:17-22

I will say unto God my rock, Why hast thou forgotten me? why go I mourning because of the oppression of the enemy?

As with a sword in my bones, mine enemies reproach me; while they say daily unto me, Where is thy God?

Why art thou cast down, O my soul? and why art thou disquieted within me? hope thou in God: for I shall yet praise him, who is the health of my countenance, and my God.

Psalms 42:9-11

The spirit of the Lord GOD is upon me; because the LORD hath anointed me to preach good tidings unto the meek; he hath sent me to bind up the brokenhearted, to proclaim liberty to the captives, and the opening of the prison to them that are bound;

To proclaim the acceptable year of the LORD, and the day of vengeance of our God; to comfort all that mourn;

Isaiah 61:1, 2

God Helps You To Forgive

This is my commandment, That ye love one another, as I have loved you.

Greater love hath no man than this, that a man lay down his life for his friends.

Ye are my friends, if ye do whatsoever I command you.

John 15:12-14

Thy kingdom come. Thy will be done in earth, as it is in heaven.

Give us this day our daily bread.

And forgive us our debts, as we forgive our debtors.

And lead us not into temptation, but deliver us from evil: For thine is the kingdom, and the power, and the glory, for ever. Amen.

For if ye forgive men their trespasses, your heavenly Father will also forgive you:

But if ye forgive not men their trespasses, neither will your Father forgive your trespasses.

Matthew 6:10-15

Therefore if thou bring thy gift to the altar, and there rememberest that thy brother hath ought against thee;

Leave there thy gift before the altar, and go thy way; first be reconciled to thy brother, and then come and offer thy gift.

Matthew 5:23, 24

Take heed to yourselves: If thy brother trespass against thee, rebuke him; and if he repent, forgive him.

And if he trespass against thee seven times in a day, and seven times in a day turn again to thee, saying, I repent; thou shalt forgive him.

Luke 17:3, 4

Him that is weak in the faith receive ye, but not to doubtful disputations.

Who art thou that judgest another man's servant? to his own master he standeth or falleth. Yea, he shall be holden up: for God is able to make him stand.

Romans 14:1, 4

Teach me thy way, O Lord, and lead me in a plain path, because of mine enemies.

Psalms 27:11

God Provides New Relationships For You

And the LORD God said, It is not good that the man should be alone; I will make him an help meet for him.

Genesis 2:18

A man that hath friends must shew himself friendly: and there is a friend that sticketh closer than a brother.

Proverbs 18:24

This is my commandment, That ye love one another, as I have loved you.

Greater love hath no man than this, that a man lay down his life for his friends.

Ye are my friends, if ye do whatsoever I command you.

Henceforth I call you not servants; for the servant knoweth not what his lord doeth: but I have called you friends; for all things that I have heard of my Father I have made known unto you.

John 15:12-15

Thou hast turned for me my mourning into dancing: thou hast put off my sackcloth, and girded me with gladness;

Psalms 30:11

He delivered me from my strong enemy, and from them which hated me: for they were too strong for me.

They prevented me in the day of my calamity: but the LORD was my stay.

He brought me forth also into a large place; he delivered me, because he delighted in me.

The LORD rewarded me according to my righteousness; according to the cleanness of my hands hath he recompensed me.

Psalms 18:17-20

When Troubles Come And You're Lonely...

God Promises To Ease The Pain

Hide not thy face far from me; put not thy servant away in anger: thou hast been my help; leave me not, neither forsake me, O God of my salvation.

Psalms 27:9

Have mercy upon me, O LORD, for I am in trouble: mine eye is consumed with grief, yea, my soul and my belly.

Psalms 31:9

The righteous cry, and the LORD heareth, and delivereth them out of all their troubles.

The LORD is nigh unto them that are of a broken heart; and saveth such as be of a contrite spirit.

Many are the afflictions of the righteous: but the LORD delivereth him out of them all.

Psalms 34:17-19

Depart from me, all ye workers of iniquity; for the LORD hath heard the voice of my weeping.

The LORD hath heard my supplication; the LORD will receive my prayer.

Psalms 6:8, 9

For it was not an enemy that reproached me; then I could have borne it: neither was it he that hated me that did magnify himself against me; then I would have hid myself from him:

But it was thou, a man mine equal, my guide, and mine acquaintance.

We took sweet counsel together, and walked unto the house of God in company.

As for me, I will call upon God; and the LORD shall save me.

Evening, and morning, and at noon, will I pray, and cry aloud: and he shall hear my voice.

He hath delivered my soul in peace from the battle that was against me: for there were many with me.

Psalms 55:12-14, 16-18

To the chief Musician upon Shoshannim, A Psalm of David. Save me, O God; for the waters are come in unto my soul.

I sink in deep mire, where there is no standing: I am come into deep waters, where the floods overflow me.

I am weary of my crying: my throat is dried: mine eyes fail while I wait for my God.

They that hate me without a cause are more than the hairs of mine head: they that would destroy me, being mine enemies wrongfully, are mighty: then I restored that which I took not away.

O God, thou knowest my foolishness; and my sins are not hid from thee.

Let not them that wait on thee, O Lord GOD of hosts, be ashamed for my sake: let not those that seek thee be confounded for my sake, O God of Israel.

Psalms 69:1-6

Praise ye the LORD: for it is good to sing praises unto our God; for it is pleasant; and praise is comely.

The LORD doth build up Jerusalem: he gathereth together the outcasts of Israel.

He healeth the broken in heart, and bindeth up their wounds.

Psalms 147:1-3

God Knows How You Feel

My friends scorn me: but mine eye poureth out tears unto God.

Job 16:20

And they came to a place which was named Gethsemane: and he saith to his disciples, Sit ye here, while I shall pray.

And he taketh with him Peter and James and John, and began to be sore amazed, and to be very heavy;

And saith unto them, My soul is exceeding sorrowful unto death: tarry ye here, and watch.

And he went forward a little, and fell on the ground, and prayed that, if it were possible, the hour might pass from him.

And he said, Abba, Father, all things are possible unto thee; take away this cup from me: nevertheless not what I will, but what thou wilt.

And he cometh, and findeth them sleeping, and saith unto Peter, Simon, sleepest thou? couldest not thou watch one hour?

Mark 14:32-37

Let Christ the King of Israel descend now from the cross, that we may see and believe. And they that were crucified with him reviled him.

And when the sixth hour was come, there was darkness over the whole land until the ninth hour.

And at the ninth hour Jesus cried with a loud voice, saying, Eloi, Eloi, lama sabachthani? which is, being interpreted, My God, my God, why hast thou forsaken me?

Mark 15:32-34

And they clothed him with purple, and platted a crown of thorns, and put it about his head,

And began to salute him, Hail, King of the Jews!

And they smote him on the head with a reed, and did spit upon him, and bowing their knees worshipped him.

And when they had mocked him, they took off the purple from him, and put his own clothes on him, and led him out to crucify him.

Mark 15:17-20

God Offers You Eternal Hope

He that dwelleth in the secret place of the most High shall abide under the shadow of the Almighty.

I will say of the LORD, He is my refuge and my fortress: my God; in him will I trust.

Psalms 91:1, 2

Why art thou cast down, O my soul? and why art thou disquieted in me? hope thou in God: for I shall yet praise him for the help of his countenance.

O my God, my soul is cast down within me: therefore will I remember thee from the land of Jordan, and of the Hermonites, from the hill Mizar.

Deep calleth unto deep at the noise of thy waterspouts: all thy waves and thy billows are gone over me.

Yet the LORD will command his loving-kindness in the daytime, and in the night his song shall be with me, and my prayer unto the God of my life.

I will say unto God my rock, Why hast thou forgotten me? why go I mourning because of the oppression of the enemy?

As with a sword in my bones, mine enemies reproach me; while they say daily unto me, Where is thy God?

Why art thou cast down, O my soul? and why art thou disquieted within me? hope thou in God: for I shall yet praise him, who is the health of my countenance, and my God.

Psalms 42:5-11

For mine enemies speak against me; and they that lay wait for my soul take counsel together,

Saying, God hath forsaken him: persecute and take him; for there is none to deliver him.

O God, be not far from me: O my God, make haste for my help.

Let them be confounded and consumed that are adversaries to my soul; let them be covered with reproach and dishonour that seek my hurt.

But I will hope continually, and will yet praise thee more and more.

Psalms 71:10-14

My soul fainteth for thy salvation: but I hope in thy word.

Mine eyes fail for thy word, saying, When wilt thou comfort me?

For I am become like a bottle in the smoke; yet do I not forget thy statutes.

Psalms 119:81-83

Happy is he that hath the God of Jacob for his help, whose hope is in the LORD his God:

Which made heaven, and earth, the sea, and all that therein is: which keepeth truth for ever:

Which executeth judgment for the oppressed: which giveth food to the hungry. The LORD looseth the prisoners:

The LORD openeth the eyes of the blind: the LORD raiseth them that are bowed down: the LORD loveth the righteous:

The LORD preserveth the strangers; he relieveth the fatherless and widow: but the way of the wicked he turneth upside down.

The LORD shall reign for ever, even thy God, O Zion, unto all generations. Praise ye the LORD.

Psalms 146:5-10

Blessed is the man that trusteth in the LORD, and whose hope the LORD is.

For he shall be as a tree planted by the waters, and that spreadeth out her roots by the river, and shall not see when heat cometh, but her leaf shall be green; and shall not be careful in the year of drought, neither shall cease from yielding fruit.

Jeremiah 17:7, 8

Why art thou cast down, O my soul? and why art thou disquieted within me? hope in God: for I shall yet praise him, who is the health of my countenance, and my God.

Psalms 43:5

When You've Matured As A Christian And Are In Fellowship...

God Gives You Directions For Guiding Younger Christians

Great is the LORD, and greatly to be praised; and his greatness is unsearchable.

One generation shall praise thy works to another, and shall declare thy mighty acts.

Psalms 145:3, 4

For he established a testimony in Jacob, and appointed a law in Israel, which he commanded our fathers, that they should make them known to their children:

That the generation to come might know them, even the children which should be born; who should arise and declare them to their children:

That they might set their hope in God, and not forget the works of God, but keep his commandments:

Psalms 78:5-7

Walk about Zion, and go round about her: tell the towers thereof.

Mark ye well her bulwarks, consider her palaces; that ye may tell it to the generation following.

Psalms 48:12, 13

I write unto you, little children, because your sins are forgiven you for his name's sake.

I write unto you, fathers, because ye have known him that is from the beginning. I write unto you, young men, because ye have overcome the wicked one. I write unto you, little children, because ye have known the Father.

I have written unto you, fathers, because ye have known him that is from the beginning. I have written unto you, young men, because ye are strong, and the word of God abideth in you, and ye have overcome the wicked one.

I John 2:12-14

Brethren, if a man be overtaken in a fault, ye which are spiritual, restore such an one in the spirit of meekness; considering thyself, lest thou also be tempted.

Bear ye one another's burdens, and so fulfil the law of Christ.

Galatians 6:1, 2

Whosoever therefore shall break one of these least commandments, and shall teach men so, he shall be called the least in the kingdom of heaven: but whosoever shall do and teach them, the same shall be called great in the kingdom of heaven.

Matthew 5:19

God Gives Responsibilities To The Elders

Remember the days of old, consider the years of many generations: ask thy father, and he will shew thee; thy elders, and they will tell thee.

Deuteronomy 32:7

And let us not be weary in well doing: for in due season we shall reap, if we faint not.

As we have therefore opportunity, let us do good unto all men, especially unto them who are of the household of faith.

Galatians 6:9, 10

The elders which are among you I exhort, who am also an elder, and a witness of the sufferings of Christ, and also a partaker of the glory that shall be revealed:

Feed the flock of God which is among you, taking the oversight thereof, not by constraint, but willingly; not for filthy lucre, but of a ready mind;

Neither as being lords over God's heritage, but being ensamples to the flock.

And when the chief Shepherd shall appear, ye shall receive a crown of glory that fadeth not away.

I Peter 5:1-4

As ye know how we exhorted and comforted and charged every one of you, as a father doth his children,

That ye would walk worthy of God, who hath called you unto his kingdom and glory.

I Thessalonians 2:11, 12

But speak thou the things which become sound doctrine:

That the aged men be sober, grave, temperate, sound in faith, in charity, in patience.

The aged women likewise, that they be in behaviour as becometh holiness, not false accusers, not given to much wine, teachers of good things;

That they may teach the young women to be sober, to love their husbands, to love their children,

To be discreet, chaste, keepers at home, good, obedient to their own husbands, that the word of God be not blasphemed.

Young men likewise exhort to be sober minded.

Titus 2:1-6

Take heed therefore unto yourselves, and to all the flock, over the which the Holy Ghost hath made you overseers, to feed the church of God, which he hath purchased with his own blood.

For I know this, that after my departing shall grievous wolves enter in among you, not sparing the flock.

Also of your own selves shall men arise, speaking perverse things, to draw away disciples after them.

Therefore watch, and remember, that by the space of three years I ceased not to warn every one night and day with tears.

Acts 20:28-31

God Asks You To Share Your Gifts

For I long to see you, that I may impart unto you some spiritual gift, to the end ye may be established;

That is, that I may be comforted together with you by the mutual faith both of you and me.

Romans 1:11, 12

Now concerning spiritual gifts, brethren, I would not have you ignorant.

Now there are diversities of gifts, but the same Spirit.

And there are differences of administrations, but the same Lord.

And there are diversities of operations, but it is the same God which worketh all in all.

I Corinthians 12:1, 4-6

For as we have many members in one body, and all members have not the same office:

So we, being many, are one body in Christ, and every one members one of another.

Having then gifts differing according to the grace that is given to us, whether prophecy, let us prophesy according to the proportion of faith;

Or ministry, let us wait on our ministering: or he that teacheth, on teaching;

Or he that exhorteth, on exhortation: he that giveth, let him do it with simplicity; he that ruleth, with diligence; he that sheweth mercy, with cheerfulness.

Let love be without dissimulation. Abhor that which is evil; cleave to that which is good.

Romans 12:4-9

And God hath set some in the church, first apostles, secondarily prophets, thirdly teachers, after that miracles, then gifts of healings, helps, governments, diversities of tongues.

Are all apostles? are all prophets? are all teachers? are all workers of miracles?

Have all the gifts of healing? do all speak with tongues? do all interpret?

But covet earnestly the best gifts: and yet shew I unto you a more excellent way.

I Corinthians 12:28-31

Follow after charity, and desire spiritual gifts, but rather that ye may prophesy.

For he that speaketh in an unknown tongue speaketh not unto men, but unto God: for no man understandeth him; howbeit in the spirit he speaketh mysteries.

But he that prophesieth speaketh unto men to edification, and exhortation, and comfort.

He that speaketh in an unknown tongue edifieth himself; but he that prophesieth edifieth the church.

I Corinthians 14:1-4

And he gave some, apostles; and some, prophets; and some, evangelists; and some, pastors and teachers;

For the perfecting of the saints, for the work of the ministry, for the edifying of the body of Christ:

Till we all come in the unity of the faith, and of the knowledge of the Son of God, unto a perfect man, unto the measure of the stature of the fulness of Christ:

That we henceforth be no more children, tossed to and fro, and carried about with every wind of doctrine, by the sleight of men, and cunning craftiness, whereby they lie in wait to deceive;

But speaking the truth in love, may grow up into him in all things, which is the head, even Christ:

From whom the whole body fitly joined together and compacted by that which every joint supplieth, according to the effectual working in the measure of every part, maketh increase of the body unto the edifying of itself in love.

Ephesians 4:11-16

When You've Matured As A Christian And Are A Community/Business Leader...

God Commands You To Be A Witness

Let your light so shine before men, that they may see your good works, and glorify your Father which is in heaven.

Matthew 5:16

How then shall they call on him in whom they have not believed? and how shall they believe in him of whom they have not heard? and how shall they hear without a preacher?

And how shall they preach, except they be sent? as it is written, How beautiful are the feet of them that preach the gospel of peace, and bring glad tidings of good things!

Romans 10:14, 15

And he said unto them, Ye are they which justify yourselves before men; but God knoweth your hearts: for that which is highly esteemed among men is abomination in the sight of God.

Luke 16:15

For nation shall rise against nation, and kingdom against kingdom: and there shall be earthquakes in divers places, and there shall be famines and troubles: these are the beginnings of sorrows.

But take heed to yourselves: for they shall deliver you up to councils; and in the synagogues ye shall be beaten: and ye shall be brought before rulers and kings for my sake, for a testimony against them.

And the gospel must first be published among all nations.

But when they shall lead you, and deliver you up, take no thought beforehand what ye shall speak, neither do ye premeditate: but whatsoever shall be given you in that hour, that speak ye: for it is not ye that speak, but the Holy Ghost.

Mark 13:8-11

And likewise he that had received two, he also gained other two.

But he that had received one went and digged in the earth, and hid his lord's money.

After a long time the lord of those servants cometh, and reckoneth with them.

And so he that had received five talents came and brought other five talents, saying, Lord, thou deliveredst unto me five talents: behold, I have gained beside them five talents more.

Matthew 25:17-20

…Thus it is written, and thus it behoved Christ to suffer, and to rise from the dead the third day:

And that repentance and remission of sins should be preached in his name among all nations, beginning at Jerusalem.

And ye are witnesses of these things.

Luke 24:46-48

God Gives Guidance In Ethical Decisions

Be ye not as the horse, or as the mule, which have no understanding: whose mouth must be held in with bit and bridle, lest they come near unto thee.

Many sorrows shall be to the wicked: but he that trusteth in the LORD, mercy shall compass him about.

Be glad in the LORD, and rejoice, ye righteous: and shout for joy, all ye that are upright in heart.

Psalms 32:9-11

A false balance is abomination to the LORD: but a just weight is his delight.

When pride cometh, then cometh shame: but with the lowly is wisdom.

The integrity of the upright shall guide them: but the perverseness of transgressors shall destroy them.

Proverbs 11:1-3

Better is a little with righteousness than great revenues without right.

A man's heart deviseth his way: but the LORD directeth his steps.

Proverbs 16:8, 9

These six things doth the LORD hate: yea, seven are an abomination unto him:

A proud look, a lying tongue, and hands that shed innocent blood,

An heart that deviseth wicked imaginations, feet that be swift in running to mischief,

A false witness that speaketh lies, and he that soweth discord among brethren.

My son, keep thy father's commandment, and forsake not the law of thy mother:

Proverbs 6:16-20

Divers weights, and divers measures, both of them are alike abomination to the LORD.

Even a child is known by his doings, whether his work be pure, and whether it be right.

Proverbs 20:10, 11

The getting of treasures by a lying tongue is a vanity tossed to and fro of them that seek death.

Proverbs 21:6

Whoso is partner with a thief hateth his own soul: he heareth cursing, and bewrayeth it not.

Proverbs 29:24

Woe unto him that buildeth his house by unrighteousness, and his chambers by wrong; that useth his neighbour's service without wages, and giveth him not for his work;

Jeremiah 22:13

Recompense to no man evil for evil. Provide things honest in the sight of all men.

Romans 12:17

Enter not into the path of the wicked, and go not in the way of evil men.

Avoid it, pass not by it, turn from it, and pass away.

For they sleep not, except they have done mischief; and their sleep is taken away, unless they cause some to fall.

For they eat the bread of wickedness, and drink the wine of violence.

But the path of the just is as the shining light, that shineth more and more unto the perfect day.

Proverbs 4:14-18

Keep thy heart with all diligence; for out of it are the issues of life.

Put away from thee a froward mouth, and perverse lips put far from thee.

Let thine eyes look right on, and let thine eyelids look straight before thee.

Ponder the path of thy feet, and let all thy ways be established.

Turn not to the right hand nor to the left: remove thy foot from evil.

Proverbs 4:23-27

God Calls You To Be Unique

For thou art an holy people unto the LORD thy God, and the LORD hath chosen thee to be a peculiar people unto himself, above all the nations that are upon the earth.

Deuteronomy 14:2

Then said one unto him, Lord, are there few that be saved? And he said unto them,

Strive to enter in at the strait gate: for many, I say unto you, will seek to enter in, and shall not be able.

Luke 13:23, 24

Then came also publicans to be baptized, and said unto him, Master, what shall we do?

And he said unto them, Exact no more than that which is appointed you.

And the soldiers likewise demanded of him, saying, And what shall we do? And he said unto them, Do violence to no man, neither accuse any falsely; and be content with your wages.

Luke 3:12-14

Then certain of the scribes and of the Pharisees answered, saying, Master, we would see a sign from thee.

But he answered and said unto them, An evil and adulterous generation seeketh after a sign; and there shall no sign be given to it, but the sign of the prophet Jonas:

For as Jonas was three days and three nights in the whale's belly; so shall the Son of man be three days and three nights in the heart of the earth.

The men of Nineveh shall rise in judgment with this generation, and shall condemn it: because they repented at the preaching of Jonas; and, behold, a greater than Jonas is here.

The queen of the south shall rise up in the judgment with this generation, and shall condemn it: for she came from the uttermost parts of the earth to hear the wisdom of Solomon; and, behold, a greater than Solomon is here.

When the unclean spirit is gone out of a man, he walketh through dry places, seeking rest, and findeth none.

Then he saith, I will return into my house from whence I came out; and when he is come, he findeth it empty, swept, and garnished.

Matthew 12:38-44

Take heed that ye do not your alms before men, to be seen of them: otherwise ye have no reward of your Father which is in heaven.

Therefore when thou doest thine alms, do not sound a trumpet before thee, as the hypocrites do in the synagogues and in the streets, that they may have glory of men. Verily I say unto you, They have their reward.

But when thou doest alms, let not thy left hand know what thy right hand doeth:

That thine alms may be in secret: and thy Father which seeth in secret himself shall reward thee openly.

Matthew 6:1-4

And seek not ye what ye shall eat, or what ye shall drink, neither be ye of doubtful mind.

For all these things do the nations of the world seek after: and your Father knoweth that ye have need of these things.

But rather seek ye the kingdom of God; and all these things shall be added unto you.

Luke 12:29-31

When You Look At Your Life And Wonder What Difference You've Made...

WHEN YOU LOOK AT YOUR LIFE AND WONDER WHAT DIFFERENCE YOU'VE MADE

God Reminds You Of The Impact Of Your Prayers

And all things, whatsoever ye shall ask in prayer, believing, ye shall receive.

Matthew 21:22

Again I say unto you, That if two of you shall agree on earth as touching any thing that they shall ask, it shall be done for them of my Father which is in heaven.

Matthew 18:19

If ye abide in me, and my words abide in you, ye shall ask what ye will, and it shall be done unto you.

John 15:7

And in that day ye shall ask me nothing. Verily, verily, I say unto you, Whatsoever ye shall ask the Father in my name, he will give it you.

John 16:23

Confess your faults one to another, and pray one for another, that ye may be healed. The effectual fervent prayer of a righteous man availeth much.

James 5:16

And I say unto you, Ask, and it shall be given you; seek, and ye shall find; knock, and it shall be opened unto you.

For every one that asketh receiveth; and he that seeketh findeth; and to him that knocketh it shall be opened.

Luke 11:9, 10

God Promises To Bring Fruit In His Season

Blessed is the man that walketh not in the counsel of the ungodly, nor standeth in the way of sinners, nor sitteth in the seat of the scornful.

But his delight is in the law of the LORD; and in his law doth he meditate day and night.

And he shall be like a tree planted by the rivers of water, that bringeth forth his fruit in his season; his leaf also shall not wither; and whatsoever he doeth shall prosper.

Psalms 1:1-3

Those that be planted in the house of the LORD shall flourish in the courts of our God.

They shall still bring forth fruit in old age; they shall be fat and flourishing;

Psalms 92:13, 14

Whoso keepeth the fig tree shall eat the fruit thereof: so he that waiteth on his master shall be honoured.

Proverbs 27:18

Ye shall know them by their fruits. Do men gather grapes of thorns, or figs of thistles?

Even so every good tree bringeth forth good fruit; but a corrupt tree bringeth forth evil fruit.

A good tree cannot bring forth evil fruit, neither can a corrupt tree bring forth good fruit.

Matthew 7:16-18

Abide in me, and I in you. As the branch cannot bear fruit of itself, except it abide in the vine; no more can ye, except ye abide in me.

I am the vine, ye are the branches: He that abideth in me, and I in him, the same bringeth forth much fruit: for without me ye can do nothing.

John 15:4, 5

Be patient therefore, brethren, unto the coming of the Lord. Behold, the husbandman waiteth for the precious fruit of the earth, and hath long patience for it, until he receive the early and latter rain.

James 5:7

God Reminds You He Only Asks For Faithfulness

And now, Israel, what doth the LORD thy God require of thee, but to fear the LORD thy God, to walk in all his ways, and to love him, and to serve the LORD thy God with all thy heart and with all thy soul,

To keep the commandments of the LORD, and his statutes, which I command thee this day for thy good?

Behold, the heaven and the heaven of heavens is the LORD'S thy God, the earth also, with all that therein is.

Deuteronomy 10:12-14

Mine eyes shall be upon the faithful of the land, that they may dwell with me: he that walketh in a perfect way, he shall serve me.

Psalms 101:6

And he said unto him, Well, thou good servant: because thou hast been faithful in a very little, have thou authority over ten cities.

Luke 19:17

I am the LORD thy God, which brought thee out of the land of Egypt: open thy mouth wide, and I will fill it.

But my people would not hearken to my voice; and Israel would none of me.

So I gave them up unto their own hearts' lust: and they walked in their own counsels.

Oh that my people had hearkened unto me, and Israel had walked in my ways!

I should soon have subdued their enemies, and turned my hand against their adversaries.

Psalms 81:10-14

Who then is a faithful and wise servant, whom his lord hath made ruler over his household, to give them meat in due season?

Blessed is that servant, whom his lord when he cometh shall find so doing.

Matthew 24:45, 46

Let a man so account of us, as of the ministers of Christ, and stewards of the mysteries of God.

Moreover it is required in stewards, that a man be found faithful.

I Corinthians 4:1, 2

When You Look At Your Life And Wonder If You've Made Mistakes...

WHEN YOU LOOK AT YOUR LIFE AND WONDER IF YOU'VE MADE MISTAKES

God Reminds You That All Have Sinned

For there is not a just man upon earth, that doeth good, and sinneth not.

Ecclesiastes 7:20

How then can man be justified with God? or how can he be clean that is born of a woman?

Behold even to the moon, and it shineth not; yea, the stars are not pure in his sight.

How much less man, that is a worm? and the son of man, which is a worm?

Job 25:4-6

Wash me throughly from mine iniquity, and cleanse me from my sin.

For I acknowledge my transgressions: and my sin is ever before me.

Against thee, thee only, have I sinned, and done this evil in thy sight: that thou mightest be justified when thou speakest, and be clear when thou judgest.

Behold, I was shapen in iniquity, and in sin did my mother conceive me.

Psalms 51:2-5

So when they continued asking him, he lifted up himself, and said unto them, He that is without sin among you, let him first cast a stone at her.

And again he stooped down, and wrote on the ground.

And they which heard it, being convicted by their own conscience, went out one by one, beginning at the eldest, even unto the last: and Jesus was left alone, and the woman standing in the midst.

When Jesus had lifted up himself, and saw none but the woman, he said unto her, Woman, where are those thine accusers? hath no man condemned thee?

She said, No man, Lord. And Jesus said unto her, Neither do I condemn thee: go, and sin no more.

John 8:7-11

If we say that we have fellowship with him, and walk in darkness, we lie, and do not the truth:

But if we walk in the light, as he is in the light, we have fellowship one with another, and the blood of Jesus Christ his Son cleanseth us from all sin.

If we say that we have no sin, we deceive ourselves, and the truth is not in us.

I John 1:6-8

As it is written, There is none righteous, no, not one:

There is none that understandeth, there is none that seeketh after God.

They are all gone out of the way, they are together become unprofitable; there is none that doeth good, no, not one.

Romans 3:10-12

God Provides The Answer To Sin

To the chief Musician, A Psalm of David, when Nathan the prophet came unto him, after he had gone in to Bath-sheba. Have mercy upon me, O God, according to thy lovingkindness: according unto the multitude of thy tender mercies blot out my transgressions.

Wash me throughly from mine iniquity, and cleanse me from my sin.

For I acknowledge my transgressions: and my sin is ever before me.

Psalms 51:1-3

I acknowledged my sin unto thee, and mine iniquity have I not hid. I said, I will confess my transgressions unto the LORD; and thou forgavest the iniquity of my sin. Selah.

Psalms 32:5

The statutes of the LORD are right, rejoicing the heart: the commandment of the LORD is pure, enlightening the eyes.

The fear of the LORD is clean, enduring for ever: the judgments of the LORD are true and righteous altogether.

More to be desired are they than gold, yea, than much fine gold: sweeter also than honey and the honeycomb.

Moreover by them is thy servant warned: and in keeping of them there is great reward.

Psalms 19:8-11

If we confess our sins, he is faithful and just to forgive us our sins, and to cleanse us from all unrighteousness.

If we say that we have not sinned, we make him a liar, and his word is not in us.

I John 1:9, 10

Finally, my brethren, be strong in the Lord, and in the power of his might.

Put on the whole armour of God, that ye may be able to stand against the wiles of the devil.

For we wrestle not against flesh and blood, but against principalities, against powers, against the rulers of the darkness of this world, against spiritual wickedness in high places.

Wherefore take unto you the whole armour of God, that ye may be able to withstand in the evil day, and having done all, to stand.

Ephesians 6:10-13

Wherefore let him that thinketh he standeth take heed lest he fall.

There hath no temptation taken you but such as is common to man: but God is faithful, who will not suffer you to be tempted above that ye are able; but will with the temptation also make a way to escape, that ye may be able to bear it.

I Corinthians 10:12, 13

God Offers You A New Beginning

Purge me with hyssop, and I shall be clean: wash me, and I shall be whiter than snow.

Make me to hear joy and gladness; that the bones which thou hast broken may rejoice.

Hide thy face from my sins, and blot out all mine iniquities.

Create in me a clean heart, O God; and renew a right spirit within me.

Psalms 51:7-10

Remember not the sins of my youth, nor my transgressions: according to thy mercy remember thou me for thy goodness' sake, O LORD.

Good and upright is the LORD: therefore will he teach sinners in the way.

Psalms 25:7, 8

Oh that men would praise the LORD for his goodness, and for his wonderful works to the children of men!

For he satisfieth the longing soul, and filleth the hungry soul with goodness.

Such as sit in darkness and in the shadow of death, being bound in affliction and iron;

Because they rebelled against the words of God, and contemned the counsel of the most High:

Therefore he brought down their heart with labour; they fell down, and there was none to help.

Then they cried unto the LORD in their trouble, and he saved them out of their distresses.

He brought them out of darkness and the shadow of death, and brake their bands in sunder.

Oh that men would praise the LORD for his goodness, and for his wonderful works to the children of men!

Psalms 107:8-15

He that covereth his sins shall not prosper: but whoso confesseth and forsaketh them shall have mercy.

Psalms 28:13

When I said, My foot slippeth; thy mercy, O LORD, held me up.

In the multitude of my thoughts within me thy comforts delight my soul.

Psalms 94:18, 19

I am become a stranger unto my brethren, and an alien unto my mother's children.

For the zeal of thine house hath eaten me up; and the reproaches of them that reproached thee are fallen upon me.

When I wept, and chastened my soul with fasting, that was to my reproach.

I made sackcloth also my garment; and I became a proverb to them.

They that sit in the gate speak against me; and I was the song of the drunkards.

But as for me, my prayer is unto thee, O LORD, in an acceptable time: O God, in the multitude of thy mercy hear me, in the truth of thy salvation.

Deliver me out of the mire, and let me not sink: let me be delivered from them that hate me, and out of the deep waters.

Hear me, O LORD; for thy lovingkindness is good: turn unto me according to the multitude of thy tender mercies.

Psalms 69:8-14, 16

Strengthen ye the weak hands, and confirm the feeble knees.

Say to them that are of a fearful heart, Be strong, fear not: behold, your God will come with vengeance, even God with a recompence; he will come and save you.

Then the eyes of the blind shall be opened, and the ears of the deaf shall be unstopped.

Then shall the lame man leap as an hart, and the tongue of the dumb sing: for in the wilderness shall waters break out, and streams in the desert.

Isaiah 35:3-6

That ye put off concerning the former conversation the old man, which is corrupt according to the deceitful lusts;

And be renewed in the spirit of your mind;

And that ye put on the new man, which after God is created in righteousness and true holiness.

Ephesians 4:22-24

When You Look At Your Life And Are Bewildered At The Evil That Surrounds You...

WHEN YOU LOOK AT YOUR LIFE AND ARE BEWILDERED AT THE EVIL THAT SURROUNDS YOU

God Reveals The Source Of Evil

For many deceivers are entered into the world, who confess not that Jesus Christ is come in the flesh. This is a deceiver and an antichrist.

Look to yourselves, that we lose not those things which we have wrought, but that we receive a full reward.

II John 1:7, 8

Be sober, be vigilant; because your adversary the devil, as a roaring lion, walketh about, seeking whom he may devour:

I Peter 5:8

A good man out of the good treasure of his heart bringeth forth that which is good; and an evil man out of the evil treasure of his heart bringeth forth that which is evil: for of the abundance of the heart his mouth speaketh.

Luke 6:45

How art thou fallen from heaven, O Lucifer, son of the morning! how art thou cut down to the ground, which didst weaken the nations!

For thou hast said in thine heart, I will ascend into heaven, I will exalt my throne above the stars of God: I will sit also upon the mount of the congregation, in the sides of the north:

I will ascend above the heights of the clouds; I will be like the most High.

Yet thou shalt be brought down to hell, to the sides of the pit.

Isaiah 14:12-15

And he shewed me Joshua the high priest standing before the angel of the LORD, and Satan standing at his right hand to resist him.

And the LORD said unto Satan, The LORD rebuke thee, O Satan; even the LORD that hath chosen Jerusalem rebuke thee: is not this a brand plucked out of the fire?

Zechariah 3:1, 2

Beloved, let us love one another: for love is of God; and every one that loveth is born of God, and knoweth God.

He that loveth not knoweth not God; for God is love.

I John 4:7, 8

WHEN YOU LOOK AT YOUR LIFE AND ARE BEWILDERED AT THE EVIL THAT SURROUNDS YOU

God Promises That Good Will Triumph

I know that, whatsoever God doeth, it shall be for ever: nothing can be put to it, nor any thing taken from it: and God doeth it, that men should fear before him.

That which hath been is now; and that which is to be hath already been; and God requireth that which is past.

And moreover I saw under the sun the place of judgment, that wickedness was there; and the place of righteousness, that iniquity was there.

I said in mine heart, God shall judge the righteous and the wicked: for there is a time there for every purpose and for every work.

Ecclesiastes 3:14-17

Though a sinner do evil an hundred times, and his days be prolonged, yet surely I know that it shall be well with them that fear God, which fear before him:

But it shall not be well with the wicked, neither shall he prolong his days, which are as a shadow; because he feareth not before God.

Ecclesiastes 8:12, 13

They have prepared a net for my steps; my soul is bowed down: they have digged a pit before me, into the midst whereof they are fallen themselves. Selah.

My heart is fixed, O God, my heart is fixed: I will sing and give praise.

Psalms 57:6, 7

And Moses said unto the people, Fear ye not, stand still, and see the salvation of the LORD, which he will shew to you today: for the Egyptians whom ye have seen today, ye shall see them again no more for ever.

The LORD shall fight for you, and ye shall hold your peace.

Exodus 14:13, 14

Then sang Moses and the children of Israel this song unto the LORD, and spake, saying, I will sing unto the LORD, for he hath triumphed gloriously: the horse and his rider hath he thrown into the sea.

The LORD is my strength and song, and he is become my salvation: he is my God, and I will prepare him an habitation; my father's God, and I will exalt him.

The LORD is a man of war: the LORD is his name.

Exodus 15:1-3

He delivered me from my strong enemy, and from them that hated me: for they were too strong for me.

They prevented me in the day of my calamity: but the LORD was my stay.

He brought me forth also into a large place: he delivered me, because he delighted in me.

II Samuel 22:18-20

Hope deferred maketh the heart sick: but when the desire cometh, it is a tree of life.

Whoso despiseth the word shall be destroyed: but he that feareth the commandment shall be rewarded.

The law of the wise is a fountain of life, to depart from the snares of death.

Good understanding giveth favour: but the way of transgressors is hard.

Proverbs 13:12-15

The LORD is far from the wicked: but he heareth the prayer of the righteous.

The light of the eyes rejoiceth the heart: and a good report maketh the bones fat.

Proverbs 15:29, 30

Who is he that overcometh the world, but he that believeth that Jesus is the Son of God?

I John 5:5

Ye are of God, little children, and have overcome them: because greater is he that is in you, than he that is in the world.

I John 4:4

WHEN YOU LOOK AT YOUR LIFE AND ARE BEWILDERED AT THE EVIL THAT SURROUNDS YOU

God Tells You How To Live With Enemies

When a man's ways please the LORD, he maketh even his enemies to be at peace with him.

Proverbs 16:7

A Psalm of David. Fret not thyself because of evildoers, neither be thou envious against the workers of iniquity.

For they shall soon be cut down like the grass, and wither as the green herb.

Psalms 37:1, 2

I will be glad and rejoice in thee: I will sing praise to thy name, O thou most High.

When mine enemies are turned back, they shall fall and perish at thy presence.

For thou hast maintained my right and my cause; thou satest in the throne judging right.

Thou hast rebuked the heathen, thou hast destroyed the wicked, thou hast put out their name for ever and ever.

O thou enemy, destructions are come to a perpetual end: and thou hast destroyed cities; their memorial is perished with them.

But the LORD shall endure for ever: he hath prepared his throne for judgment.

And he shall judge the world in righteousness, he shall minister judgment to the people in uprightness.

The LORD also will be a refuge for the oppressed, a refuge in times of trouble.

Psalms 9:2-9

Happy art thou, O Israel: who is like unto thee, O people saved by the LORD, the shield of thy help, and who is the sword of thy excellency! and thine enemies shall be found liars unto thee; and thou shalt tread upon their high places.

Deuteronomy 33:29

The merciful man doeth good to his own soul: but he that is cruel troubleth his own flesh.

The wicked worketh a deceitful work: but to him that soweth righteousness shall be a sure reward.

As righteousness tendeth to life: so he that pursueth evil pursueth it to his own death.

Proverbs 11:17-19

Say not thou, I will recompense evil; but wait on the LORD, and he shall save thee.

Proverbs 20:22

Ye have heard that it hath been said, Thou shalt love thy neighbour, and hate thine enemy.

But I say unto you, Love your enemies, bless them that curse you, do good to them that hate you, and pray for them which despitefully use you, and persecute you;

That ye may be the children of your Father which is in heaven: for he maketh his sun to rise on the evil and on the good, and sendeth rain on the just and on the unjust.

For if ye love them which love you, what reward have ye? do not even the publicans the same?

And if ye salute your brethren only, what do ye more than others? do not even the publicans so?

Be ye therefore perfect, even as your Father which is in heaven is perfect.

Matthew 5:43-48

When You Experience God's Fruit And Know Joy...

God Promises Joy Through Tribulation

He will swallow up death in victory; and the Lord GOD will wipe away tears from off all faces; and the rebuke of his people shall he take away from off all the earth: for the LORD hath spoken it.

And it shall be said in that day, Lo, this is our God; we have waited for him, and he will save us: this is the LORD; we have waited for him, we will be glad and rejoice in his salvation.

Isaiah 25:8, 9

They that sow in tears shall reap in joy.

He that goeth forth and weepeth, bearing precious seed, shall doubtless come again with rejoicing, bringing his sheaves with him.

Psalms 126:5, 6

Therefore the redeemed of the LORD shall return, and come with singing unto Zion; and everlasting joy shall be upon their head: they shall obtain gladness and joy; and sorrow and mourning shall flee away.

Isaiah 51:11

Remember the word that I said unto you, The servant is not greater than his lord. If they have persecuted me, they will also persecute you; if they have kept my saying, they will keep yours also.

But when the Comforter is come, whom I will send unto you from the Father, even the Spirit of truth, which proceedeth from the Father, he shall testify of me:

And ye also shall bear witness, because ye have been with me from the beginning.

John 15:20, 26, 27

Great is my boldness of speech toward you, great is my glorying of you: I am filled with comfort, I am exceeding joyful in all our tribulation.

For, when we were come into Macedonia, our flesh had no rest, but we were troubled on every side; without were fightings, within were fears.

Nevertheless God, that comforteth those that are cast down, comforted us by the coming of Titus;

II Corinthians 7:4-6

The LORD liveth; and blessed be my rock; and let the God of my salvation be exalted.

It is God that avengeth me, and subdueth the people under me.

He delivereth me from mine enemies: yea, thou liftest me up above those that rise up against me: thou hast delivered me from the violent man.

Therefore will I give thanks unto thee, O LORD, among the heathen, and sing praises unto thy name.

Psalms 18:46-49

And the ransomed of the LORD shall return, and come to Zion with songs and everlasting joy upon their heads: they shall obtain joy and gladness, and sorrow and sighing shall flee away.

Isaiah 35:10

God Promises Joy Based On His Boundless Love

Blessed is the people that know the joyful sound: they shall walk, O LORD, in the light of thy countenance.

Psalms 89:15

But let all those that put their trust in thee rejoice: let them ever shout for joy, because thou defendest them: let them also that love thy name be joyful in thee.

For thou, LORD, wilt bless the righteous; with favour wilt thou compass him as with a shield.

Psalms 5:11, 12

Then a cloud covered the tent of the congregation, and the glory of the LORD filled the tabernacle.

And Moses was not able to enter into the tent of the congregation, because the cloud abode thereon, and the glory of the LORD filled the tabernacle.

Exodus 40:34, 35

A Song and Psalm for the sons of Korah. Great is the LORD, and greatly to be praised in the city of our God, in the mountain of his holiness.

Beautiful for situation, the joy of the whole earth, is mount Zion, on the sides of the north, the city of the great King.

Psalms 48:1, 2

He that handleth a matter wisely shall find good: and whoso trusteth in the LORD, happy is he.

Proverbs 16:20

And in that day thou shalt say, O LORD, I will praise thee: though thou wast angry with me, thine anger is turned away, and thou comfortedst me.

Behold, God is my salvation; I will trust, and not be afraid: for the LORD JEHOVAH is my strength and my song; he also is become my salvation.

Isaiah 12:1, 2

These things have I spoken unto you, that my joy might remain in you, and that your joy might be full.

John 15:11

God Promises Joy That Lasts Forever

And the ransomed of the LORD shall return, and come to Zion with songs and everlasting joy upon their heads: they shall obtain joy and gladness, and sorrow and sighing shall flee away.

Isaiah 35:10

A Psalm of praise. Make a joyful noise unto the LORD, all ye lands.

Serve the LORD with gladness: come before his presence with singing.

Psalms 100:1, 2

Therefore the redeemed of the LORD shall return, and come with singing unto Zion; and everlasting joy shall be upon their head: they shall obtain gladness and joy; and sorrow and mourning shall flee away.

Isaiah 51:11

For with God nothing shall be impossible.

Luke 1:37

I will greatly rejoice in the LORD, my soul shall be joyful in my God; for he hath clothed me with the garments of salvation, he hath covered me with the robe of righteousness, as a bridegroom decketh himself with ornaments, and as a bride adorneth herself with her jewels.

For as the earth bringeth forth her bud, and as the garden causeth the things that are sown in it to spring forth; so the Lord GOD will cause righteousness and praise to spring forth before all the nations.

Isaiah 61:10, 11

A woman when she is in travail hath sorrow, because her hour is come: but as soon as she is delivered of the child, she remembereth no more the anguish, for joy that a man is born into the world.

And ye now therefore have sorrow: but I will see you again, and your heart shall rejoice, and your joy no man taketh from you.

John 16:21, 22

When You Experience God's Fruit And Know Peace...

God Fills You With His Peace

Rejoice in the Lord alway: and again I say, Rejoice.

Let your moderation be known unto all men. The Lord is at hand.

Be careful for nothing; but in every thing by prayer and supplication with thanksgiving let your requests be made known unto God.

And the peace of God, which passeth all understanding, shall keep your hearts and minds through Christ Jesus.

Philippians 4:4-7

My son, forget not my law; but let thine heart keep my commandments:

For length of days, and long life, and peace, shall they add to thee.

Proverbs 3:1, 2

The word which God sent unto the children of Israel, preaching peace by Jesus Christ: (he is Lord of all:)

Acts 10:36

Therefore being justified by faith, we have peace with God through our Lord Jesus Christ:

Romans 5:1

To all that be in Rome, beloved of God, called to be saints: Grace to you and peace from God our Father, and the Lord Jesus Christ.

Romans 1:7

Thou hast put gladness in my heart, more than in the time that their corn and their wine increased.

I will both lay me down in peace, and sleep: for thou, LORD, only makest me dwell in safety.

Psalms 4:7, 8

God Blesses You When You Seek Peace

Blessed are the peacemakers: for they shall be called the children of God.

Matthew 5:9

Depart from evil, and do good; seek peace, and pursue it.

Psalms 34:14

Great peace have they which love thy law: and nothing shall offend them.

Psalms 119:165

Finally, brethren, whatsoever things are true, whatsoever things are honest, whatsoever things are just, whatsoever things are pure, whatsoever things are lovely, whatsoever things are of good report; if there be any virtue, and if there be any praise, think on these things.

Those things, which ye have both learned, and received, and heard, and seen in me, do: and the God of peace shall be with you.

Philippians 4:8, 9

The LORD will give strength unto his people; the LORD will bless his people with peace.

Psalms 29:11

For ye shall go out with joy, and be led forth with peace: the mountains and the hills shall break forth before you into singing, and all the trees of the field shall clap their hands.

Isaiah 55:12

God Gives You Peace In Troubled Times

Thou wilt keep him in perfect peace, whose mind is stayed on thee: because he trusteth in thee.

Isaiah 26:3

To the chief Musician, Al-taschith, Michtam of David, when he fled from Saul in the cave. Be merciful unto me, O God, be merciful unto me: for my soul trusteth in thee: yea, in the shadow of thy wings will I make my refuge, until these calamities be overpast.

I will cry unto God most high; unto God that performeth all things for me.

Psalms 57:1, 2

Now no chastening for the present seemeth to be joyous, but grievous: nevertheless afterward it yieldeth the peaceable fruit of righteousness unto them which are exercised thereby.

Hebrews 12:11

Through the tender mercy of our God; whereby the dayspring from on high hath visited us,

To give light to them that sit in darkness and in the shadow of death, to guide our feet into the way of peace.

Luke 1:78, 79

When a man's ways please the LORD, he maketh even his enemies to be at peace with him.

Proverbs 16:7

The LORD of hosts is with us; the God of Jacob is our refuge. Selah.

Come, behold the works of the LORD, what desolations he hath made in the earth.

He maketh wars to cease unto the end of the earth; he breaketh the bow, and cutteth the spear in sunder; he burneth the chariot in the fire.

Be still, and know that I am God: I will be exalted among the heathen, I will be exalted in the earth.

The LORD of hosts is with us; the God of Jacob is our refuge. Selah.

Psalms 46:7-11

When You Experience God's Fruit And Know Brotherly Love...

God Shows You How To Love Others More

And thou shalt love the Lord thy God with all thy heart, and with all thy soul, and with all thy mind, and with all thy strength: this is the first commandment.

And the second is like, namely this, Thou shalt love thy neighbour as thyself. There is none other commandment greater than these.

And the scribe said unto him, Well, Master, thou hast said the truth: for there is one God; and there is none other but he:

And to love him with all the heart, and with all the understanding, and with all the soul, and with all the strength, and to love his neighbour as himself, is more than all whole burnt offerings and sacrifices.

And when Jesus saw that he answered discreetly, he said unto him, Thou art not far from the kingdom of God. And no man after that durst ask him any question.

Mark 12:30-34

Let love be without dissimulation. Abhor that which is evil; cleave to that which is good.

Be kindly affectioned one to another with brotherly love; in honour preferring one another;

Romans 12:9, 10

For scarcely for a righteous man will one die: yet peradventure for a good man some would even dare to die.

But God commendeth his love toward us, in that, while we were yet sinners, Christ died for us.

Romans 5:7, 8

A friend loveth at all times, and a brother is born for adversity.

Proverbs 17:17

For I say, through the grace given unto me, to every man that is among you, not to think of himself more highly than he ought to think; but to think soberly, according as God hath dealt to every man the measure of faith.

Romans 12:3

Love worketh no ill to his neighbour: therefore love is the fulfilling of the law.

Romans 13:10

Finally, be ye all of one mind, having compassion one of another, love as brethren, be pitiful, be courteous:

Not rendering evil for evil, or railing for railing: but contrariwise blessing; knowing that ye are thereunto called, that ye should inherit a blessing.

For he that will love life, and see good days, let him refrain his tongue from evil, and his lips that they speak no guile:

Let him eschew evil, and do good; let him seek peace, and ensue it.

For the eyes of the Lord are over the righteous, and his ears are open unto their prayers: but the face of the Lord is against them that do evil.

I Peter 3:8-12

God Blesses You When You Share Yourself

We give thanks to God and the Father of our Lord Jesus Christ, praying always for you,

Since we heard of your faith in Christ Jesus, and of the love which ye have to all the saints,

For the hope which is laid up for you in heaven, whereof ye heard before in the word of the truth of the gospel;

Colossians 1:3-5

Blessed be the God and Father of our Lord Jesus Christ, who hath blessed us with all spiritual blessings in heavenly places in Christ:

According as he hath chosen us in him before the foundation of the world, that we should be holy and without blame before him in love:

Ephesians 1:3, 4

Peace be to the brethren, and love with faith, from God the Father and the Lord Jesus Christ.

Grace be with all them that love our Lord Jesus Christ in sincerity. Amen.

Ephesians 6:23, 24

And this I pray, that your love may abound yet more and more in knowledge and in all judgment;

That ye may approve things that are excellent; that ye may be sincere and without offence till the day of Christ;

Being filled with the fruits of righteousness, which are by Jesus Christ, unto the glory and praise of God.

Philippians 1:9-11

Beloved, let us love one another: for love is of God; and every one that loveth is born of God, and knoweth God.

He that loveth not knoweth not God; for God is love.

In this was manifested the love of God toward us, because that God sent his only begotten Son into the world, that we might live through him.

Herein is love, not that we loved God, but that he loved us, and sent his Son to be the propitiation for our sins.

Beloved, if God so loved us, we ought also to love one another.

I John 4:7-11

Two are better than one; because they have a good reward for their labour.

For if they fall, the one will lift up his fellow: but woe to him that is alone when he falleth; for he hath not another to help him up.

Again, if two lie together, then they have heat: but how can one be warm alone?

And if one prevail against him, two shall withstand him; and a threefold cord is not quickly broken.

Ecclesiastes 4:9-12

God Fills His Children With Love

Who shall separate us from the love of Christ? shall tribulation, or distress, or persecution, or famine, or nakedness, or peril, or sword?

As it is written, For thy sake we are killed all the day long; we are accounted as sheep for the slaughter.

Nay, in all these things we are more than conquerors through him that loved us.

For I am persuaded, that neither death, nor life, nor angels, nor principalities, nor powers, nor things present, nor things to come,

Nor height, nor depth, nor any other creature, shall be able to separate us from the love of God, which is in Christ Jesus our Lord.

Romans 8:35-39

For this cause I bow my knees unto the Father of our Lord Jesus Christ,

Of whom the whole family in heaven and earth is named,

That he would grant you, according to the riches of his glory, to be strengthened with might by his Spirit in the inner man;

That Christ may dwell in your hearts by faith; that ye, being rooted and grounded in love,

May be able to comprehend with all saints what is the breadth, and length, and depth, and height;

And to know the love of Christ, which passeth knowledge, that ye might be filled with all the fulness of God.

Ephesians 3:14-19

Now God himself and our Father, and our Lord Jesus Christ, direct our way unto you.

And the Lord make you to increase and abound in love one toward another, and toward all men, even as we do toward you:

I Thessalonians 3:11, 12

If a man say, I love God, and hateth his brother, he is a liar: for he that loveth not his brother whom he hath seen, how can he love God whom he hath not seen?

And this commandment have we from him, That he who loveth God love his brother also.

I John 4:20, 21

Whosoever believeth that Jesus is the Christ is born of God: and every one that loveth him that begat loveth him also that is begotten of him.

By this we know that we love the children of God, when we love God, and keep his commandments.

For this is the love of God, that we keep his commandments: and his commandments are not grievous.

For whatsoever is born of God overcometh the world: and this is the victory that overcometh the world, even our faith.

I John 5:1-4

When You Experience God's Fruit And Know Faith...

God Promises To Increase Your Faith

Looking unto Jesus the author and finisher of our faith; who for the joy that was set before him endured the cross, despising the shame, and is set down at the right hand of the throne of God.

Hebrews 12:2

Jesus said unto him, If thou canst believe, all things are possible to him that believeth.

And straightway the father of the child cried out, and said with tears, Lord, I believe; help thou mine unbelief.

Mark 9:23, 24

But the manifestation of the Spirit is given to every man to profit withal.

For to one is given by the Spirit the word of wisdom; to another the word of knowledge by the same Spirit;

To another faith by the same Spirit; to another the gifts of healing by the same Spirit;

I Corinthians 12:7-9

And my speech and my preaching was not with enticing words of man's wisdom, but in demonstration of the Spirit and of power:

That your faith should not stand in the wisdom of men, but in the power of God.

I Corinthians 2:4, 5

Mercy unto you, and peace and love, be multiplied.

Beloved, when I gave all diligence to write unto you of the common salvation, it was needful for me to write unto you, and exhort you that ye should earnestly contend for the faith which was once delivered unto the saints.

Jude 1:2, 3

And the apostles said unto the Lord, Increase our faith.

And the Lord said, If ye had faith as a grain of mustard seed, ye might say unto this sycamine tree, Be thou plucked up by the root, and be thou planted in the sea; and it should obey you.

Luke 17:5, 6

God Promises To Reward Your Faith

O love the LORD, all ye his saints: for the LORD preserveth the faithful, and plentifully rewardeth the proud doer.

Be of good courage, and he shall strengthen your heart, all ye that hope in the LORD.

Psalms 31:23, 24

And Jesus answering saith unto them, Have faith in God.

For verily I say unto you, That whosoever shall say unto this mountain, Be thou removed, and be thou cast into the sea; and shall not doubt in his heart, but shall believe that those things which he saith shall come to pass; he shall have whatsoever he saith.

Therefore I say unto you, What things soever ye desire, when ye pray, believe that ye receive them, and ye shall have them.

Mark 11:22-24

Now faith is the substance of things hoped for, the evidence of things not seen.

For by it the elders obtained a good report.

Through faith we understand that the worlds were framed by the word of God, so that things which are seen were not made of things which do appear.

Hebrews 11:1-3

And when he saw a fig tree in the way, he came to it, and found nothing thereon, but leaves only, and said unto it, Let no fruit grow on thee henceforward for ever. And presently the fig tree withered away.

And when the disciples saw it, they marvelled, saying, How soon is the fig tree withered away!

Jesus answered and said unto them, Verily I say unto you, If ye have faith, and doubt not, ye shall not only do this which is done to the fig tree, but also if ye shall say unto this mountain, Be thou removed, and be thou cast into the sea; it shall be done.

Matthew 21:19-21

Then Jesus answered and said unto her, O woman, great is thy faith: be it unto thee even as thou wilt. And her daughter was made whole from that very hour.

Matthew 15:28

The LORD is nigh unto all them that call upon him, to all that call upon him in truth.

He will fulfil the desire of them that fear him: he also will hear their cry, and will save them.

The LORD preserveth all them that love him: but all the wicked will he destroy.

Psalms 145:18-20

God Interacts With Your Faith

And he did not many mighty works there because of their unbelief.

Matthew 13:58

By faith Abel offered unto God a more excellent sacrifice than Cain, by which he obtained witness that he was righteous, God testifying of his gifts: and by it he being dead yet speaketh.

By faith Enoch was translated that he should not see death; and was not found, because God had translated him: for before his translation he had this testimony, that he pleased God.

But without faith it is impossible to please him: for he that cometh to God must believe that he is, and that he is a rewarder of them that diligently seek him.

By faith Noah, being warned of God of things not seen as yet, moved with fear, prepared an ark to the saving of his house; by the which he condemned the world, and became heir of the righteousness which is by faith.

Hebrews 11:4-7

By faith Moses, when he was come to years, refused to be called the son of Pharaoh's daughter;

Choosing rather to suffer affliction with the people of God, than to enjoy the pleasures of sin for a season;

Esteeming the reproach of Christ greater riches than the treasures in Egypt: for he had respect unto the recompence of the reward.

By faith he forsook Egypt, not fearing the wrath of the king: for he endured, as seeing him who is invisible.

Through faith he kept the passover, and the sprinkling of blood, lest he that destroyed the firstborn should touch them.

By faith they passed through the Red sea as by dry land: which the Egyptians assaying to do were drowned.

By faith the walls of Jericho fell down, after they were compassed about seven days.

By faith the harlot Rahab perished not with them that believed not, when she had received the spies with peace.

Hebrews 11:24-31

And, behold, a woman, which was diseased with an issue of blood twelve years, came behind him, and touched the hem of his garment:

For she said within herself, If I may but touch his garment, I shall be whole.

But Jesus turned him about, and when he saw her, he said, Daughter, be of good comfort; thy faith hath made thee whole. And the woman was made whole from that hour.

Matthew 9:20-22

And when Jesus departed thence, two blind men followed him, crying, and saying, Thou son of David, have mercy on us.

And when he was come into the house, the blind men came to him: and Jesus saith unto them, Believe ye that I am able to do this? They said unto him, Yea, Lord.

Then touched he their eyes, saying, According to your faith be it unto you.

Matthew 9:27-29

Even so faith, if it hath not works, is dead, being alone.

Yea, a man may say, Thou hast faith, and I have works: shew me thy faith without thy works, and I will shew thee my faith by my works.

Thou believest that there is one God; thou doest well: the devils also believe, and tremble.

But wilt thou know, O vain man, that faith without works is dead?

James 2:17-20

When You Look At Your Future And Ask About Death...

WHEN YOU LOOK AT YOUR FUTURE AND ASK ABOUT DEATH

God Promises To Be With You Now And Forever

When the waves of death compassed me, the floods of ungodly men made me afraid;

The sorrows of hell compassed me about; the snares of death prevented me;

In my distress I called upon the LORD, and cried to my God: and he did hear my voice out of his temple, and my cry did enter into his ears.

II Samuel 22:5-7

Consider and hear me, O LORD my God: lighten mine eyes, lest I sleep the sleep of death;

Lest mine enemy say, I have prevailed against him; and those that trouble me rejoice when I am moved.

But I have trusted in thy mercy; my heart shall rejoice in thy salvation.

I will sing unto the LORD, because he hath dealt bountifully with me.

Psalms 13:3-6

As for me, I will behold thy face in righteousness: I shall be satisfied, when I awake, with thy likeness.

Psalms 17:15

Yea, though I walk through the valley of the shadow of death, I will fear no evil: for thou art with me; thy rod and thy staff they comfort me.

Psalms 23:4

A Psalm of David. The LORD is my light and my salvation; whom shall I fear? the LORD is the strength of my life; of whom shall I be afraid?

Psalms 27:1

Is there not an appointed time to man upon earth? are not his days also like the days of an hireling?

As a servant earnestly desireth the shadow, and as an hireling looketh for the reward of his work:

So am I made to possess months of vanity, and wearisome nights are appointed to me.

Job 7:1-3

For this God is our God for ever and ever: he will be our guide even unto death.

Psalms 48:14

My soul, wait thou only upon God; for my expectation is from him.

Psalms 62:5

A Psalm of David, when he was in the wilderness of Judah. O God, thou art my God; early will I seek thee: my soul thirsteth for thee, my flesh longeth for thee in a dry and thirsty land, where no water is;

To see thy power and thy glory, so as I have seen thee in the sanctuary.

Because thy lovingkindness is better than life, my lips shall praise thee.

Psalms 63:1-3

Whither shall I go from thy spirit? or whither shall I flee from thy presence?

If I ascend up into heaven, thou art there: if I make my bed in hell, behold, thou art there.

If I take the wings of the morning, and dwell in the uttermost parts of the sea;

Even there shall thy hand lead me, and thy right hand shall hold me.

Psalms 139:7-10

WHEN YOU LOOK AT YOUR FUTURE AND ASK ABOUT DEATH

God Gives You Eternal Life

He asked life of thee, and thou gavest it him, even length of days for ever and ever.

His glory is great in thy salvation: honour and majesty hast thou laid upon him.

For thou hast made him most blessed for ever: thou hast made him exceeding glad with thy countenance.

For the king trusteth in the LORD, and through the mercy of the most High he shall not be moved.

Psalms 21:4-7

But God will redeem my soul from the power of the grave: for he shall receive me. Selah.

Psalms 49:15

For I know that my redeemer liveth, and that he shall stand at the latter day upon the earth:

And though after my skin worms destroy this body, yet in my flesh shall I see God:

Job 19:25, 26

For the wages of sin is death; but the gift of God is eternal life through Jesus Christ our Lord.

Romans 6:23

To the chief Musician, Maschil, for the sons of Korah. As the hart panteth after the water brooks, so panteth my soul after thee, O God.

My soul thirsteth for God, for the living God: when shall I come and appear before God?

Psalms 42:1, 2

In a moment, in the twinkling of an eye, at the last trump: for the trumpet shall sound, and the dead shall be raised incorruptible, and we shall be changed.

For this corruptible must put on incorruption, and this mortal must put on immortality.

So when this corruptible shall have put on incorruption, and this mortal shall have put on immortality, then shall be brought to pass the saying that is written, Death is swallowed up in victory.

O death, where is thy sting? O grave, where is thy victory?

I Corinthians 15:52-55

God Will Comfort Your Loved Ones

For I will pour water upon him that is thirsty, and floods upon the dry ground: I will pour my spirit upon thy seed, and my blessing upon thine offspring:

Isaiah 44:3

A father of the fatherless, and a judge of the widows, is God in his holy habitation.

Psalms 68:5

He shall feed his flock like a shepherd: he shall gather the lambs with his arm, and carry them in his bosom, and shall gently lead those that are with young.

Isaiah 40:11

For the Lord hath comforted his people, and will have mercy upon his afflicted.

Isaiah 49:13b

Blessed are they that mourn: for they shall be comforted.

Matthew 5:4

As one whom his mother comforteth, so will I comfort you; and ye shall be comforted in Jerusalem.

Isaiah 66:13

And they that know thy name will put their trust in thee: for thou, LORD, hast not forsaken them that seek thee.

Psalms 9:10

When You Look At Your Future And Wonder About Retirement...

God Reminds You Your Identity Is Not With Your Job

Now when he had left speaking, he said unto Simon, Launch out into the deep, and let down your nets for a draught.

And Simon answering said unto him, Master, we have toiled all the night, and have taken nothing: nevertheless at thy word I will let down the net.

And when they had this done, they inclosed a great multitude of fishes: and their net brake.

And they beckoned unto their partners, which were in the other ship, that they should come and help them. And they came, and filled both the ships, so that they began to sink.

When Simon Peter saw it, he fell down at Jesus' knees, saying, Depart from me; for I am a sinful man, O Lord.

For he was astonished, and all that were with him, at the draught of the fishes which they had taken:

And so was also James, and John, the sons of Zebedee, which were partners with Simon. And Jesus said unto Simon, Fear not; from henceforth thou shalt catch men.

And when they had brought their ships to land, they forsook all, and followed him.

Luke 5:4-11

The words of the Preacher, the son of David, king in Jerusalem.

Vanity of vanities, saith the Preacher, vanity of vanities; all is vanity.

What profit hath a man of all his labour which he taketh under the sun?

One generation passeth away, and another generation cometh: but the earth abideth for ever.

Ecclesiastes 1:1-4

Therefore I hated life; because the work that is wrought under the sun is grievous unto me: for all is vanity and vexation of spirit.

Yea, I hated all my labour which I had taken under the sun: because I should leave it unto the man that shall be after me.

And who knoweth whether he shall be a wise man or a fool? yet shall he have rule over all my labour wherein I have laboured, and wherein I have shewed myself wise under the sun. This is also vanity.

Ecclesiastes 2:17-19

Then Satan answered the LORD, and said, Doth Job fear God for nought?

Hast not thou made an hedge about him, and about his house, and about all that he hath on every side? thou hast blessed the work of his hands, and his substance is increased in the land.

But put forth thine hand now, and touch all that he hath, and he will curse thee to thy face.

And the LORD said unto Satan, Behold, all that he hath is in thy power; only upon himself put not forth thine hand. So Satan went forth from the presence of the LORD.

Then Job arose, and rent his mantle, and shaved his head, and fell down upon the ground, and worshipped,

And said, Naked came I out of my mother's womb, and naked shall I return thither: the LORD gave, and the LORD hath taken away; blessed be the name of the LORD.

In all this Job sinned not, nor charged God foolishly.

Job 1:9-12, 20-22

WHEN YOU LOOK AT YOUR FUTURE AND WONDER ABOUT RETIREMENT

God Gives Your Life New Meaning

Oh let the wickedness of the wicked come to an end; but establish the just: for the righteous God trieth the hearts and reins.

I will praise the LORD according to his righteousness: and will sing praise to the name of the LORD most high.

Psalms 7:9, 17

I am forgotten as a dead man out of mind: I am like a broken vessel.

But I trusted in thee, O LORD: I said, Thou art my God.

Psalms 31:12, 14

The word which came to Jeremiah from the LORD, saying,

Arise, and go down to the potter's house, and there I will cause thee to hear my words.

Then I went down to the potter's house, and, behold, he wrought a work on the wheels.

And the vessel that he made of clay was marred in the hand of the potter: so he made it again another vessel, as seemed good to the potter to make it.

Then the word of the LORD came to me, saying,

O house of Israel, cannot I do with you as this potter? saith the LORD. Behold, as the clay is in the potter's hand, so are ye in mine hand, O house of Israel.

Jeremiah 18:1-6

But God forbid that I should glory, save in the cross of our Lord Jesus Christ, by whom the world is crucified unto me, and I unto the world;

Galatians 6:14

Now therefore ye are no more strangers and foreigners, but fellowcitizens with the saints, and of the household of God;

And are built upon the foundation of the apostles and prophets, Jesus Christ himself being the chief corner stone;

In whom all the building fitly framed together groweth unto an holy temple in the Lord:

In whom ye also are builded together for an habitation of God through the Spirit.

Ephesians 2:19-22

Hear, O LORD, and have mercy upon me: LORD, be thou my helper.

Thou hast turned for me my mourning into dancing: thou hast put off my sackcloth, and girded me with gladness;

To the end that my glory may sing praise to thee, and not be silent. O LORD my God, I will give thanks unto thee for ever.

Psalms 30:10-12

WHEN YOU LOOK AT YOUR FUTURE AND WONDER ABOUT RETIREMENT

God Walks With You

To the chief Musician upon Neginah, A Psalm of David. Hear my cry, O God; attend unto my prayer.

From the end of the earth will I cry unto thee, when my heart is overwhelmed: lead me to the rock that is higher than I.

For thou hast been a shelter for me, and a strong tower from the enemy.

I will abide in thy tabernacle for ever: I will trust in the covert of thy wings. Selah.

For thou, O God, hast heard my vows: thou hast given me the heritage of those that fear thy name.

Psalms 61:1-5

Nevertheless I am continually with thee: thou hast holden me by my right hand.

Thou shalt guide me with thy counsel, and afterward receive me to glory.

Psalms 73:23, 24

...Preserve me, O God: for in thee do I put my trust.

Psalms 16:1

LORD, make me to know mine end, and the measure of my days, what it is; that I may know how frail I am.

Behold, thou hast made my days as an handbreadth; and mine age is as nothing before thee: verily every man at his best state is altogether vanity.

And now, Lord, what wait I for? my hope is in thee.

Psalms 39:4, 5, 7

I love the LORD, because he hath heard my voice and my supplications.

Because he hath inclined his ear unto me, therefore will I call upon him as long as I live.

The sorrows of death compassed me, and the pains of hell gat hold upon me: I found trouble and sorrow.

Then called I upon the name of the LORD; O LORD, I beseech thee, deliver my soul.

Gracious is the LORD, and righteous; yea, our God is merciful.

Psalms 116:1-5

Therefore we are always confident, knowing that, whilst we are at home in the body, we are absent from the Lord:

(For we walk by faith, not by sight:)

We are confident, I say, and willing rather to be absent from the body, and to be present with the Lord.

Wherefore we labour, that, whether present or absent, we may be accepted of him.

II Corinthians 5:6-9

When You Look At Your Future And Worry About Your Family...

WHEN YOU LOOK AT YOUR FUTURE AND WORRY ABOUT YOUR FAMILY

God Promises To Be With Them

I have been young, and now am old; yet have I not seen the righteous forsaken, nor his seed begging bread.

He is ever merciful, and lendeth; and his seed is blessed.

Depart from evil, and do good; and dwell for evermore.

For the LORD loveth judgment, and forsaketh not his saints; they are preserved for ever: but the seed of the wicked shall be cut off.

The righteous shall inherit the land, and dwell therein for ever.

Psalms 37:25-29

Thou shalt know also that thy seed shall be great, and thine offspring as the grass of the earth.

Thou shalt come to thy grave in a full age, like as a shock of corn cometh in in his season.

Lo this, we have searched it, so it is; hear it, and know thou it for thy good.

Job 5:25-27

For the LORD your God is God of gods, and Lord of lords, a great God, a mighty, and a terrible, which regardeth not persons, nor taketh reward:

He doth execute the judgment of the fatherless and widow, and loveth the stranger, in giving him food and raiment.

Deuteronomy 10:17, 18

Ye shall not afflict any widow, or fatherless child.

If thou afflict them in any wise, and they cry at all unto me, I will surely hear their cry;

Exodus 22:22, 23

And Moses was an hundred and twenty years old when he died: his eye was not dim, nor his natural force abated.

And the children of Israel wept for Moses in the plains of Moab thirty days: so the days of weeping and mourning for Moses were ended.

And Joshua the son of Nun was full of the spirit of wisdom; for Moses had laid his hands upon him: and the children of Israel hearkened unto him, and did as the LORD commanded Moses.

Deuteronomy 34:7-9

Now there cried a certain woman of the wives of the sons of the prophets unto Elisha, saying, Thy servant my husband is dead; and thou knowest that thy servant did fear the LORD: and the creditor is come to take unto him my two sons to be bondmen.

And Elisha said unto her, What shall I do for thee? tell me, what hast thou in the house? And she said, Thine handmaid hath not any thing in the house, save a pot of oil.

Then he said, Go, borrow thee vessels abroad of all thy neighbours, even empty vessels; borrow not a few.

And when thou art come in, thou shalt shut the door upon thee and upon thy sons, and shalt pour out into all those vessels, and thou shalt set aside that which is full.

So she went from him, and shut the door upon her and upon her sons, who brought the vessels to her; and she poured out.

And it came to pass, when the vessels were full, that she said unto her son, Bring me yet a vessel. And he said unto her, There is not a vessel more. And the oil stayed.

Then she came and told the man of God. And he said, Go, sell the oil, and pay thy debt, and live thou and thy children of the rest.

II Kings 4:1-7

He shall judge the poor of the people, he shall save the children of the needy, and shall break in pieces the oppressor.

Psalms 72:4

For God will save Zion, and will build the cities of Judah: that they may dwell there, and have it in possession.

The seed also of his servants shall inherit it: and they that love his name shall dwell therein.

Psalms 69:35, 36

Praise ye the LORD. Blessed is the man that feareth the LORD, that delighteth greatly in his commandments.

His seed shall be mighty upon earth: the generation of the upright shall be blessed.

Wealth and riches shall be in his house: and his righteousness endureth for ever.

Psalms 112:1-3

Children's children are the crown of old men; and the glory of children are their fathers.

Proverbs 17:6

And it shall be unto them for an inheritance: I am their inheritance: and ye shall give them no possession in Israel: I am their possession.

Ezekiel 44:28

God Promises To Answer Your Prayers

The children of thy servants shall continue, and their seed shall be established before thee.

Psalms 102:28

Delight thyself also in the LORD; and he shall give thee the desires of thine heart.

Commit thy way unto the LORD; trust also in him; and he shall bring it to pass.

Psalms 37:4, 5

For I will set mine eyes upon them for good, and I will bring them again to this land: and I will build them, and not pull them down; and I will plant them, and not pluck them up.

And I will give them an heart to know me, that I am the LORD: and they shall be my people, and I will be their God: for they shall return unto me with their whole heart.

Jeremiah 24:6, 7

Blessed be the LORD, because he hath heard the voice of my supplications.

Psalms 28:6

To the chief Musician, A Psalm of David. The king shall joy in thy strength, O LORD; and in thy salvation how greatly shall he rejoice!

Thou hast given him his heart's desire, and hast not withholden the request of his lips. Selah.

Psalms 21:1, 2

And said, I beseech thee, O LORD God of heaven, the great and terrible God, that keepeth covenant and mercy for them that love him and observe his commandments:

Let thine ear now be attentive, and thine eyes open, that thou mayest hear the prayer of thy servant, which I pray before thee now, day and night, for the children of Israel thy servants, and confess the sins of the children of Israel, which we have sinned against thee: both I and my father's house have sinned.

We have dealt very corruptly against thee, and have not kept the commandments, nor the statutes, nor the judgments, which thou commandedst thy servant Moses.

Remember, I beseech thee, the word that thou commandedst thy servant Moses, saying, If ye transgress, I will scatter you abroad among the nations:

But if ye turn unto me, and keep my commandments, and do them; though there were of you cast out unto the uttermost part of the heaven, yet will I gather them from thence, and will bring them unto the place that I have chosen to set my name there.

Now these are thy servants and thy people, whom thou hast redeemed by thy great power, and by thy strong hand.

O Lord, I beseech thee, let now thine ear be attentive to the prayer of thy servant, and to the prayer of thy servants, who desire to fear thy name: and prosper, I pray thee, thy servant this day, and grant him mercy in the sight of this man. For I was the king's cupbearer.

Nehemiah 1:5-11

And all things, whatsoever ye shall ask in prayer, believing, ye shall receive.

Matthew 21:22

WHEN YOU LOOK AT YOUR FUTURE AND WORRY ABOUT YOUR FAMILY

God Expands Your Family Through Others

Then Peter began to say unto him, Lo, we have left all, and have followed thee.

And Jesus answered and said, Verily I say unto you, There is no man that hath left house, or brethren, or sisters, or father, or mother, or wife, or children, or lands, for my sake, and the gospel's,

But he shall receive an hundredfold now in this time, houses, and brethren, and sisters, and mothers, and children, and lands, with persecutions; and in the world to come eternal life.

Mark 10:28-30

Behold, what manner of love the Father hath bestowed upon us, that we should be called the sons of God: therefore the world knoweth us not, because it knew him not.

I John 3:1

For this cause I bow my knees unto the Father of our Lord Jesus Christ,

Of whom the whole family in heaven and earth is named,

Ephesians 3:14, 15

For thy Maker is thine husband; the LORD of hosts is his name; and thy Redeemer the Holy One of Israel; The God of the whole earth shall he be called.

Isaiah 54:5

The elder unto the elect lady and her children, whom I love in the truth; and not I only, but also all they that have known the truth;

I rejoiced greatly that I found of thy children walking in truth, as we have received a commandment from the Father.

And now I beseech thee, lady, not as though I wrote a new commandment unto thee, but that which we had from the beginning, that we love one another.

II John 1:1, 4, 5

And he answered them, saying, Who is my mother, or my brethren?

And he looked round about on them which sat about him, and said, Behold my mother and my brethren!

For whosoever shall do the will of God, the same is my brother, and my sister, and mother.

Mark 3:33-35

When You Reach The Peak Of Your Life And Are Feeling Secure...

WHEN YOU REACH THE PEAK OF YOUR LIFE AND ARE FEELING SECURE

God Commands You To Remember Him

I would seek unto God, and unto God would I commit my cause:

Which doeth great things and unsearchable; marvellous things without number:

Who giveth rain upon the earth, and sendeth waters upon the fields:

To set up on high those that be low; that those which mourn may be exalted to safety.

He disappointeth the devices of the crafty, so that their hands cannot perform their enterprise.

He taketh the wise in their own craftiness: and the counsel of the froward is carried headlong.

Job 5:8-13

For the LORD knoweth the way of the righteous: but the way of the ungodly shall perish.

Psalms 1:6

Now therefore fear the LORD, and serve him in sincerity and in truth: and put away the gods which your fathers served on the other side of the flood, and in Egypt; and serve ye the LORD.

And if it seem evil unto you to serve the LORD, choose you this day whom ye will serve; whether the gods which your fathers served that were on the other side of the flood, or the gods of the Amorites, in whose land ye dwell: but as for me and my house, we will serve the LORD.

Joshua 24:14, 15

Honour the LORD with thy substance, and with the firstfruits of all thine increase:

So shall thy barns be filled with plenty, and thy presses shall burst out with new wine.

Proverbs 3:9, 10

Better is the poor that walketh in his uprightness, than he that is perverse in his ways, though he be rich.

Proverbs 28:6

But he answered and said, It is written, Man shall not live by bread alone, but by every word that proceedeth out of the mouth of God.

Matthew 4:4

There is nothing better for a man, than that he should eat and drink, and that he should make his soul enjoy good in his labour. This also I saw, that it was from the hand of God.

For who can eat, or who else can hasten hereunto, more than I?

For God giveth to a man that is good in his sight wisdom, and knowledge, and joy: but to the sinner he giveth travail, to gather and to heap up, that he may give to him that is good before God. This also is vanity and vexation of spirit.

Ecclesiastes 2:24-26

For the Son of man is as a man taking a far journey, who left his house, and gave authority to his servants, and to every man his work, and commanded the porter to watch.

Watch ye therefore: for ye know not when the master of the house cometh, at even, or at midnight, or at the cockcrowing, or in the morning:

Lest coming suddenly he find you sleeping.

And what I say unto you I say unto all, Watch.

Mark 13:34-37

Consider the work of God: for who can make that straight, which he hath made crooked?

In the day of prosperity be joyful, but in the day of adversity consider: God also hath set the one over against the other, to the end that man should find nothing after him.

Ecclesiastes 7:13, 14

God Shows You The Real Meaning Of Security

Their inward thought is, that their houses shall continue for ever, and their dwelling places to all generations; they call their lands after their own names.

Nevertheless man being in honour abideth not: he is like the beasts that perish.

This their way is their folly: yet their posterity approve their sayings. Selah.

Psalms 49:11-13

The LORD is the portion of mine inheritance and of my cup: thou maintainest my lot.

The lines are fallen unto me in pleasant places; yea, I have a goodly heritage.

I will bless the LORD, who hath given me counsel: my reins also instruct me in the night seasons.

I have set the LORD always before me: because he is at my right hand, I shall not be moved.

Therefore my heart is glad, and my glory rejoiceth: my flesh also shall rest in hope.

Psalms 16:5-9

One dieth in his full strength, being wholly at ease and quiet.

His breasts are full of milk, and his bones are moistened with marrow.

And another dieth in the bitterness of his soul, and never eateth with pleasure.

They shall lie down alike in the dust, and the worms shall cover them.

Job 21:23-26

Thou art my hiding place; thou shalt preserve me from trouble; thou shalt compass me about with songs of deliverance. Selah.

Psalms 32:7

And of Benjamin he said, The beloved of the Lord shall dwell in safety by him: and the Lord shall cover him all the day long, and he shall dwell between his shoulders.

Deuteronomy 33:12

For promotion cometh neither from the east, nor from the west, nor from the south.

But God is the judge: he putteth down one, and setteth up another.

Psalms 75:6, 7

A Song of degrees for Solomon. Except the LORD build the house, they labour in vain that build it: except the LORD keep the city, the watchman waketh but in vain.

Psalms 127:1

The LORD will not suffer the soul of the righteous to famish: but he casteth away the substance of the wicked.

Proverbs 10:3

Better is little with the fear of the LORD than great treasure and trouble therewith.

Proverbs 15:16

Lay not up for yourselves treasures upon earth, where moth and rust doth corrupt, and where thieves break through and steal:

But lay up for yourselves treasures in heaven, where neither moth nor rust doth corrupt, and where thieves do not break through nor steal:

Matthew 6:19, 20

God Reminds You How To Treat Others

He that despiseth his neighbour sinneth: but he that hath mercy on the poor, happy is he.

He that oppresseth the poor reproacheth his Maker: but he that honoureth him hath mercy on the poor.

Proverbs 14:21, 31

It is as sport to a fool to do mischief: but a man of understanding hath wisdom.

The fear of the wicked, it shall come upon him: but the desire of the righteous shall be granted.

As the whirlwind passeth, so is the wicked no more: but the righteous is an everlasting foundation.

As vinegar to the teeth, and as smoke to the eyes, so is the sluggard to them that send him.

The fear of the LORD prolongeth days: but the years of the wicked shall be shortened.

Proverbs 10:23-27

Whoso rewardeth evil for good, evil shall not depart from his house.

Proverbs 17:13

He that hath a bountiful eye shall be blessed; for he giveth of his bread to the poor.

Proverbs 22:9

For whosoever exalteth himself shall be abased; and he that humbleth himself shall be exalted.

Then said he also to him that bade him, When thou makest a dinner or a supper, call not thy friends, nor thy brethren, neither thy kinsmen, nor thy rich neighbours; lest they also bid thee again, and a recompence be made thee.

But when thou makest a feast, call the poor, the maimed, the lame, the blind:

And thou shalt be blessed; for they cannot recompense thee: for thou shalt be recompensed at the resurrection of the just.

Luke 14:11-14

When You Reach The Peak Of Your Life And Are Financially Stable...

God Asks You To Share With Others

Give to every man that asketh of thee; and of him that taketh away thy goods ask them not again.

And as ye would that men should do to you, do ye also to them likewise.

For if ye love them which love you, what thank have ye? for sinners also love those that love them.

And if ye do good to them which do good to you, what thank have ye? for sinners also do even the same.

And if ye lend to them of whom ye hope to receive, what thank have ye? for sinners also lend to sinners, to receive as much again.

But love ye your enemies, and do good, and lend, hoping for nothing again; and your reward shall be great, and ye shall be the children of the Highest: for he is kind unto the unthankful and to the evil.

Luke 6:30-35

Take heed that ye do not your alms before men, to be seen of them: otherwise ye have no reward of your Father which is in heaven.

Therefore when thou doest thine alms, do not sound a trumpet before thee, as the hypocrites do in the synagogues and in the streets, that they may have glory of men. Verily I say unto you, They have their reward.

But when thou doest alms, let not thy left hand know what thy right hand doeth:

That thine alms may be in secret: and thy Father which seeth in secret himself shall reward thee openly.

Matthew 6:1-4

Withhold not good from them to whom it is due, when it is in the power of thine hand to do it.

Say not unto thy neighbour, Go, and come again, and to morrow I will give; when thou hast it by thee.

Proverbs 3:27, 28

The sleep of a labouring man is sweet, whether he eat little or much: but the abundance of the rich will not suffer him to sleep.

There is a sore evil which I have seen under the sun, namely, riches kept for the owners thereof to their hurt.

Ecclesiastes 5:12, 13

Herein is our love made perfect, that we may have boldness in the day of judgment: because as he is, so are we in this world.

I John 4:17

If there be among you a poor man of one of thy brethren within any of thy gates in thy land which the LORD thy God giveth thee, thou shalt not harden thine heart, nor shut thine hand from thy poor brother:

But thou shalt open thine hand wide unto him, and shalt surely lend him sufficient for his need, in that which he wanteth.

Deuteronomy 15:7, 8

Fear not, little flock; for it is your Father's good pleasure to give you the kingdom.

Sell that ye have, and give alms; provide yourselves bags which wax not old, a treasure in the heavens that faileth not, where no thief approacheth, neither moth corrupteth.

For where your treasure is, there will your heart be also.

Luke 12:32-34

WHEN YOU REACH THE PEAK OF YOUR LIFE AND ARE FINANCIALLY STABLE

God Reminds You That With Money Comes Responsibility

And he said unto them, Take heed, and beware of covetousness: for a man's life consisteth not in the abundance of the things which he possesseth.

Luke 12:15

Every way of a man is right in his own eyes: but the LORD pondereth the hearts.

To do justice and judgment is more acceptable to the LORD than sacrifice.

Proverbs 21:2, 3

There is a sore evil which I have seen under the sun, namely, riches kept for the owners thereof to their hurt.

But those riches perish by evil travail: and he begetteth a son, and there is nothing in his hand.

As he came forth of his mother's womb, naked shall he return to go as he came, and shall take nothing of his labour, which he may carry away in his hand.

And this also is a sore evil, that in all points as he came, so shall he go: and what profit hath he that hath laboured for the wind?

Ecclesiastes 5:13-16

Whoso stoppeth his ears at the cry of the poor, he also shall cry himself, but shall not be heard.

Proverbs 21:13

Give to him that asketh thee, and from him that would borrow of thee turn not thou away.

Matthew 5:42

Now when he had left speaking, he said unto Simon, Launch out into the deep, and let down your nets for a draught.

And Simon answering said unto him, Master, we have toiled all the night, and have taken nothing: nevertheless at thy word I will let down the net.

And when they had this done, they inclosed a great multitude of fishes: and their net brake.

And they beckoned unto their partners, which were in the other ship, that they should come and help them. And they came, and filled both the ships, so that they began to sink.

When Simon Peter saw it, he fell down at Jesus' knees, saying, Depart from me; for I am a sinful man, O Lord.

Luke 5:4-8

WHEN YOU REACH THE PEAK OF YOUR LIFE AND ARE FINANCIALLY STABLE

God Reminds You He Is The Source Of All Good Things

God shall likewise destroy thee for ever, he shall take thee away, and pluck thee out of thy dwelling place, and root thee out of the land of the living. Selah.

The righteous also shall see, and fear, and shall laugh at him:

Lo, this is the man that made not God his strength; but trusted in the abundance of his riches, and strengthened himself in his wickedness.

But I am like a green olive tree in the house of God: I trust in the mercy of God for ever and ever.

I will praise thee for ever, because thou hast done it: and I will wait on thy name; for it is good before thy saints.

Psalms 52:5-9

A faithful man shall abound with blessings: but he that maketh haste to be rich shall not be innocent.

To have respect of persons is not good: for for a piece of bread that man will transgress.

He that hasteth to be rich hath an evil eye, and considereth not that poverty shall come upon him.

Proverbs 28:20-22

To the chief Musician, A Psalm for the sons of Korah. O clap your hands, all ye people; shout unto God with the voice of triumph.

For the LORD most high is terrible; he is a great King over all the earth.

Psalms 47:1, 2

Then I looked on all the works that my hands had wrought, and on the labour that I had laboured to do: and, behold, all was vanity and vexation of spirit, and there was no profit under the sun.

And I turned myself to behold wisdom, and madness, and folly: for what can the man do that cometh after the king? even that which hath been already done.

Then I saw that wisdom excelleth folly, as far as light excelleth darkness.

Ecclesiastes 2:11-13

Behold that which I have seen: it is good and comely for one to eat and to drink, and to enjoy the good of all his labour that he taketh under the sun all the days of his life, which God giveth him: for it is his portion.

Every man also to whom God hath given riches and wealth, and hath given him power to eat thereof, and to take his portion, and to rejoice in his labour; this is the gift of God.

For he shall not much remember the days of his life; because God answereth him in the joy of his heart.

Ecclesiastes 5:18-20

I the LORD search the heart, I try the reins, even to give every man according to his ways, and according to the fruit of his doings.

As the partridge sitteth on eggs, and hatcheth them not; so he that getteth riches, and not by right, shall leave them in the midst of his days, and at his end shall be a fool.

Jeremiah 17:10, 11

When You Reach The Peak Of Your Life And Are Content…

God Cautions You About Complacency

An horse is a vain thing for safety: neither shall he deliver any by his great strength.

Behold, the eye of the LORD is upon them that fear him, upon them that hope in his mercy;

To deliver their soul from death, and to keep them alive in famine.

Our soul waiteth for the LORD: he is our help and our shield.

Psalms 33:17-20

Boast not thyself of to morrow; for thou knowest not what a day may bring forth.

Proverbs 27:1

Labour not to be rich: cease from thine own wisdom.

Wilt thou set thine eyes upon that which is not? for riches certainly make themselves wings; they fly away as an eagle toward heaven.

Proverbs 23:4, 5

Go to the ant, thou sluggard; consider her ways, and be wise:

Which having no guide, overseer, or ruler,

Provideth her meat in the summer, and gathereth her food in the harvest.

How long wilt thou sleep, O sluggard? when wilt thou arise out of thy sleep?

Yet a little sleep, a little slumber, a little folding of the hands to sleep:

So shall thy poverty come as one that travelleth, and thy want as an armed man.

Proverbs 6:6-11

A good name is rather to be chosen than great riches, and loving favour rather than silver and gold.

The rich and poor meet together: the LORD is the maker of them all.

A prudent man foreseeth the evil, and hideth himself: but the simple pass on, and are punished.

Proverbs 22:1-3

Be thou diligent to know the state of thy flocks, and look well to thy herds.

For riches are not for ever: and doth the crown endure to every generation?

Proverbs 27:23, 24

Two things have I required of thee; deny me them not before I die:

Remove far from me vanity and lies: give me neither poverty nor riches; feed me with food convenient for me:

Lest I be full, and deny thee, and say, Who is the LORD? or lest I be poor, and steal, and take the name of my God in vain.

Proverbs 30:7-9

God Challenges You To Take Risks

It is God that girdeth me with strength, and maketh my way perfect.

He maketh my feet like hinds' feet, and setteth me upon my high places.

He teacheth my hands to war, so that a bow of steel is broken by mine arms.

Thou hast also given me the shield of thy salvation: and thy right hand hath holden me up, and thy gentleness hath made me great.

Thou hast enlarged my steps under me, that my feet did not slip.

Psalms 18:32-36

For thou wilt light my candle: the LORD my God will enlighten my darkness.

For by thee I have run through a troop; and by my God have I leaped over a wall.

Psalms 18:28, 29

Thou wilt shew me the path of life: in thy presence is fulness of joy; at thy right hand there are pleasures for evermore.

Psalms 16:11

Shadrach, Meshach, and Abed-nego, answered and said to the king, O Nebuchadnezzar, we are not careful to answer thee in this matter.

If it be so, our God whom we serve is able to deliver us from the burning fiery furnace, and he will deliver us out of thine hand, O king.

But if not, be it known unto thee, O king, that we will not serve thy gods, nor worship the golden image which thou hast set up.

The LORD God is my strength, and he will make my feet like hinds' feet, and he will make me to walk upon mine high places. To the chief singer on my stringed instruments.

Daniel 3:16-19

And when he had called the people unto him with his disciples also, he said unto them, Whosoever will come after me, let him deny himself, and take up his cross, and follow me.

For whosoever will save his life shall lose it; but whosoever shall lose his life for my sake and the gospel's, the same shall save it.

For what shall it profit a man, if he shall gain the whole world, and lose his own soul?

Mark 8:34-36

The LORD God is my strength, and he will make my feet like hinds feet, and he will make me to walk upon mine high places. To the chief singer on my stringed instruments.

Habakkuk 3:19

WHEN YOU REACH THE PEAK OF YOUR LIFE AND ARE CONTENT

God Continues To Refine Your New Opportunities

The fear of the LORD is clean, enduring for ever: the judgments of the LORD are true and righteous altogether.

More to be desired are they than gold, yea, than much fine gold: sweeter also than honey and the honeycomb.

Moreover by them is thy servant warned: and in keeping of them there is great reward.

Who can understand his errors? cleanse thou me from secret faults.

Psalms 19:9-12

Thou hast made the earth to tremble; thou hast broken it: heal the breaches thereof; for it shaketh.

Thou hast shewed thy people hard things: thou hast made us to drink the wine of astonishment.

Thou hast given a banner to them that fear thee, that it may be displayed because of the truth. Selah.

Psalms 60:2-4

Come, and let us return unto the LORD: for he hath torn, and he will heal us; he hath smitten, and he will bind us up.

Hosea 6:1

Awake, O sword, against my shepherd, and against the man that is my fellow, saith the LORD of hosts: smite the shepherd, and the sheep shall be scattered: and I will turn mine hand upon the little ones.

And it shall come to pass, that in all the land, saith the LORD, two parts therein shall be cut off and die; but the third shall be left therein.

And I will bring the third part through the fire, and will refine them as silver is refined, and will try them as gold is tried: they shall call on my name, and I will hear them: I will say, It is my people: and they shall say, The LORD is my God.

Zechariah 13:7-9

Judge not, that ye be not judged.

For with what judgment ye judge, ye shall be judged: and with what measure ye mete, it shall be measured to you again.

And why beholdest thou the mote that is in thy brother's eye, but considerest not the beam that is in thine own eye?

Or how wilt thou say to thy brother, Let me pull out the mote out of thine eye; and, behold, a beam is in thine own eye?

Thou hypocrite, first cast out the beam out of thine own eye; and then shalt thou see clearly to cast out the mote out of thy brother's eye.

Matthew 7:1-5

I beseech you therefore, brethren, by the mercies of God, that ye present your bodies a living sacrifice, holy, acceptable unto God, which is your reasonable service.

And be not conformed to this world: but be ye transformed by the renewing of your mind, that ye may prove what is that good, and acceptable, and perfect, will of God.

Matthew 12:1, 2

When You Know Your Needs And Ask For Wisdom...

God Reminds You Of The Frailty Of The World's Wisdom

Let no man deceive himself. If any man among you seemeth to be wise in this world, let him become a fool, that he may be wise.

For the wisdom of this world is foolishness with God. For it is written, He taketh the wise in their own craftiness.

I Corinthians 3:18, 19

For the preaching of the cross is to them that perish foolishness; but unto us which are saved it is the power of God.

For it is written, I will destroy the wisdom of the wise, and will bring to nothing the understanding of the prudent.

Where is the wise? where is the scribe? where is the disputer of this world? hath not God made foolish the wisdom of this world?

For after that in the wisdom of God the world by wisdom knew not God, it pleased God by the foolishness of preaching to save them that believe.

For the Jews require a sign, and the Greeks seek after wisdom:

But we preach Christ crucified, unto the Jews a stumblingblock, and unto the Greeks foolishness;

But unto them which are called, both Jews and Greeks, Christ the power of God, and the wisdom of God.

Because the foolishness of God is wiser than men; and the weakness of God is stronger than men.

I Corinthians 1:18-25

He disappointeth the devices of the crafty, so that their hands cannot perform their enterprise.

He taketh the wise in their own craftiness: and the counsel of the froward is carried headlong.

They meet with darkness in the daytime, and grope in the noonday as in the night.

Job 5:12-14

I have seen all the works that are done under the sun; and, behold, all is vanity and vexation of spirit.

That which is crooked cannot be made straight: and that which is wanting cannot be numbered.

I communed with mine own heart, saying, Lo, I am come to great estate, and have gotten more wisdom than all they that have been before me in Jerusalem: yea, my heart had great experience of wisdom and knowledge.

And I gave my heart to know wisdom, and to know madness and folly: I perceived that this also is vexation of spirit.

For in much wisdom is much grief: and he that increaseth knowledge increaseth sorrow.

Ecclesiastes 1:14-18

Whoso despiseth the word shall be destroyed: but he that feareth the commandment shall be rewarded.

The law of the wise is a fountain of life, to depart from the snares of death.

Good understanding giveth favour: but the way of transgressors is hard.

Every prudent man dealeth with knowledge: but a fool layeth open his folly.

A wicked messenger falleth into mischief: but a faithful ambassador is health.

Poverty and shame shall be to him that refuseth instruction: but he that regardeth reproof shall be honoured.

The desire accomplished is sweet to the soul: but it is abomination to fools to depart from evil.

He that walketh with wise men shall be wise: but a companion of fools shall be destroyed.

Proverbs 13:13-20

Woe unto them that call evil good, and good evil; that put darkness for light, and light for darkness; that put bitter for sweet, and sweet for bitter!

Woe unto them that are wise in their own eyes, and prudent in their own sight!

Isaiah 5:20, 21

God Promises To Give You Wisdom From Above

Get wisdom, get understanding: forget it not; neither decline from the words of my mouth.

Forsake her not, and she shall preserve thee: love her, and she shall keep thee.

Wisdom is the principal thing; therefore get wisdom: and with all thy getting get understanding.

Exalt her, and she shall promote thee: she shall bring thee to honour, when thou dost embrace her.

She shall give to thine head an ornament of grace: a crown of glory shall she deliver to thee.

Hear, O my son, and receive my sayings; and the years of thy life shall be many.

I have taught thee in the way of wisdom; I have led thee in right paths.

Proverbs 4:5-11

The proverbs of Solomon the son of David, king of Israel;

To know wisdom and instruction; to perceive the words of understanding;

To receive the instruction of wisdom, justice, and judgment, and equity;

To give subtilty to the simple, to the young man knowledge and discretion.

A wise man will hear, and will increase learning; and a man of understanding shall attain unto wise counsels:

To understand a proverb, and the interpretation; the words of the wise, and their dark sayings.

The fear of the LORD is the beginning of knowledge: but fools despise wisdom and instruction.

Proverbs 1:1-7

Reprove not a scorner, lest he hate thee: rebuke a wise man, and he will love thee.

Give instruction to a wise man, and he will be yet wiser: teach a just man, and he will increase in learning.

The fear of the LORD is the beginning of wisdom: and the knowledge of the holy is understanding.

For by me thy days shall be multiplied, and the years of thy life shall be increased.

Proverbs 9:8-11

I wisdom dwell with prudence, and find out knowledge of witty inventions.

The fear of the LORD is to hate evil: pride, and arrogancy, and the evil way, and the froward mouth, do I hate.

Counsel is mine, and sound wisdom: I am understanding; I have strength.

By me kings reign, and princes decree justice.

By me princes rule, and nobles, even all the judges of the earth.

I love them that love me; and those that seek me early shall find me.

Proverbs 8:12-17

Give therefore thy servant an understanding heart to judge thy people, that I may discern between good and bad: for who is able to judge this thy so great a people?

And the speech pleased the Lord, that Solomon had asked this thing.

And God said unto him, Because thou hast asked this thing, and hast not asked for thyself long life; neither hast asked riches for thyself, nor hast asked the life of thine enemies; but hast asked for thyself understanding to discern judgment;

Behold, I have done according to thy words: lo, I have given thee a wise and an understanding heart; so that there was none like thee before thee, neither after thee shall any arise like unto thee.

I Kings 3:9-12

And the LORD spake unto Moses, saying,

And I have filled him with the spirit of God, in wisdom, and in understanding, and in knowledge, and in all manner of workmanship,

To devise cunning works, to work in gold, and in silver, and in brass,

And in cutting of stones, to set them, and in carving of timber, to work in all manner of workmanship.

Exodus 31:1, 3-5

At that time Jesus answered and said, I thank thee, O Father, Lord of heaven and earth, because thou hast hid these things from the wise and prudent, and hast revealed them unto babes.

Matthew 11:25

God Gives You The Definition Of True Wisdom

There was a little city, and few men within it; and there came a great king against it, and besieged it, and built great bulwarks against it:

Now there was found in it a poor wise man, and he by his wisdom delivered the city; yet no man remembered that same poor man.

Then said I, Wisdom is better than strength: nevertheless the poor man's wisdom is despised, and his words are not heard.

The words of wise men are heard in quiet more than the cry of him that ruleth among fools.

Wisdom is better than weapons of war: but one sinner destroyeth much good.

Ecclesiastes 9:14-18

O LORD, how manifold are thy works! in wisdom hast thou made them all: the earth is full of thy riches.

Psalms 104:24

The law of the LORD is perfect, converting the soul: the testimony of the LORD is sure, making wise the simple.

Psalms 19:7

Better is a poor and a wise child than an old and foolish king, who will no more be admonished.

Ecclesiastes 4:13

He that trusteth in his riches shall fall: but the righteous shall flourish as a branch.

He that troubleth his own house shall inherit the wind: and the fool shall be servant to the wise of heart.

The fruit of the righteous is a tree of life; and he that winneth souls is wise.

Proverbs 11:28-30

Only the LORD give thee wisdom and understanding, and give thee charge concerning Israel, that thou mayest keep the law of the LORD thy God.

Then shalt thou prosper, if thou takest heed to fulfil the statutes and judgments which the LORD charged Moses with concerning Israel: be strong, and of good courage; dread not, nor be dismayed.

I Chronicles 22:12, 13

When You Know Your Needs And Ask For Courage...

God Provides Courage When You Need It Most

Hast thou not known? hast thou not heard, that the everlasting God, the LORD, the Creator of the ends of the earth, fainteth not, neither is weary? there is no searching of his understanding.

He giveth power to the faint; and to them that have no might he increaseth strength.

Even the youths shall faint and be weary, and the young men shall utterly fall:

But they that wait upon the LORD shall renew their strength; they shall mount up with wings as eagles; they shall run, and not be weary; and they shall walk, and not faint.

Isaiah 40:28-31

Thy shoes shall be iron and brass; and as thy days, so shall thy strength be.

There is none like unto the God of Jeshurun, who rideth upon the heaven in thy help, and in his excellency on the sky.

The eternal God is thy refuge, and underneath are the everlasting arms: and he shall thrust out the enemy from before thee; and shall say, Destroy them.

Deuteronomy 33:25-27

There shall not any man be able to stand before thee all the days of thy life: as I was with Moses, so I will be with thee: I will not fail thee, nor forsake thee.

Be strong and of a good courage: for unto this people shalt thou divide for an inheritance the land, which I sware unto their fathers to give them.

Joshua 1:5-6

And he gave Joshua the son of Nun a charge, and said, Be strong and of a good courage: for thou shalt bring the children of Israel into the land which I sware unto them: and I will be with thee.

Deuteronomy 31:23

And from thence, when the brethren heard of us, they came to meet us as far as Appii forum, and The three taverns: whom when Paul saw, he thanked God, and took courage.

Acts 28:15

It is God that girdeth me with strength, and maketh my way perfect.

He maketh my feet like hinds' feet, and setteth me upon my high places.

He teacheth my hands to war, so that a bow of steel is broken by mine arms.

Thou hast also given me the shield of thy salvation: and thy right hand hath holden me up, and thy gentleness hath made me great.

Psalms 18:32-35

God Goes With You

To the chief Musician for the sons of Korah, A Song upon Alamoth. God is our refuge and strength, a very present help in trouble.

Therefore will not we fear, though the earth be removed, and though the mountains be carried into the midst of the sea;

Though the waters thereof roar and be troubled, though the mountains shake with the swelling thereof. Selah.

Psalms 46:1-3

Be strong and of a good courage, fear not, nor be afraid of them: for the LORD thy God, he it is that doth go with thee; he will not fail thee, nor forsake thee.

Deuteronomy 31:6

There shall no evil befall thee, neither shall any plague come nigh thy dwelling.

For he shall give his angels charge over thee, to keep thee in all thy ways.

Psalms 91:10, 11

A Song of degrees. I will lift up mine eyes unto the hills, from whence cometh my help.

My help cometh from the LORD, which made heaven and earth.

He will not suffer thy foot to be moved: he that keepeth thee will not slumber.

Behold, he that keepeth Israel shall neither slumber nor sleep.

The LORD is thy keeper: the LORD is thy shade upon thy right hand.

The sun shall not smite thee by day, nor the moon by night.

The LORD shall preserve thee from all evil: he shall preserve thy soul.

The LORD shall preserve thy going out and thy coming in from this time forth, and even for evermore.

Psalms 121:1-8

Have not I commanded thee? Be strong and of a good courage; be not afraid, neither be thou dismayed: for the LORD thy God is with thee whithersoever thou goest.

Joshua 1:9

Trust in the LORD with all thine heart; and lean not unto thine own understanding.

In all thy ways acknowledge him, and he shall direct thy paths.

Be not wise in thine own eyes: fear the LORD, and depart from evil.

Proverbs 3:5-7

God Defeats Your Fears

To the chief Musician, A Psalm of David, the servant of the LORD, who spake unto the LORD the words of this song in the day that the LORD delivered him from the hand of all his enemies, and from the hand of Saul: And he said, I will love thee, O LORD, my strength.

The LORD is my rock, and my fortress, and my deliverer; my God, my strength, in whom I will trust; my buckler, and the horn of my salvation, and my high tower.

I will call upon the LORD, who is worthy to be praised: so shall I be saved from mine enemies.

Psalms 18:1-3

And the LORD, he it is that doth go before thee; he will be with thee, he will not fail thee, neither forsake thee: fear not, neither be dismayed.

Deuteronomy 31:8

The eternal God is thy refuge, and underneath are the everlasting arms: and he shall thrust out the enemy from before thee; and shall say, Destroy them.

Deuteronomy 33:27

A Psalm of David. The LORD is my light and my salvation; whom shall I fear? the LORD is the strength of my life; of whom shall I be afraid?

Psalms 27:1

I sought the LORD, and he heard me, and delivered me from all my fears.

They looked unto him, and were lightened: and their faces were not ashamed.

This poor man cried, and the LORD heard him, and saved him out of all his troubles.

The angel of the LORD encampeth round about them that fear him, and delivereth them.

O taste and see that the LORD is good: blessed is the man that trusteth in him.

O fear the LORD, ye his saints: for there is no want to them that fear him.

Psalms 34:4-9

When thou liest down, thou shalt not be afraid: yea, thou shalt lie down, and thy sleep shall be sweet.

Be not afraid of sudden fear, neither of the desolation of the wicked, when it cometh.

For the LORD shall be thy confidence, and shall keep thy foot from being taken.

Proverbs 3:24-26

When You Know Your Needs And Humble Yourself Before God...

God Rewards The Meek

The meek shall eat and be satisfied: they shall praise the LORD that seek him: your heart shall live for ever.

Psalms 22:26

Arise, O LORD; O God, lift up thine hand: forget not the humble.

LORD, thou hast heard the desire of the humble: thou wilt prepare their heart, thou wilt cause thine ear to hear:

Psalms 10:12, 17

A Psalm of David, when he changed his behaviour before Abimelech; who drove him away, and he departed. I will bless the LORD at all times: his praise shall continually be in my mouth.

My soul shall make her boast in the LORD: the humble shall hear thereof, and be glad.

Psalms 34:1, 2

The meek will he guide in judgment: and the meek will he teach his way.

Psalms 25:9

Pride goeth before destruction, and an haughty spirit before a fall.

Better it is to be of an humble spirit with the lowly, than to divide the spoil with the proud.

Proverbs 16:18, 19

But the meek shall inherit the earth; and shall delight themselves in the abundance of peace.

Psalms 37:11

Praise him with the timbrel and dance: praise him with stringed instruments and organs.

Psalms 150:4

Whosoever therefore shall humble himself as this little child, the same is greatest in the kingdom of heaven.

Matthew 18:4

Blessed are the meek: for they shall inherit the earth.

Matthew 5:5

God Reminds You Of Your Beginning

And the LORD God formed man of the dust of the ground, and breathed into his nostrils the breath of life; and man became a living soul.

Genesis 2:7

All flesh shall perish together, and man shall turn again unto dust.

Job 34:15

For he remembered that they were but flesh; a wind that passeth away, and cometh not again.

Psalms 78:39

Then the LORD answered Job out of the whirlwind, and said,

Who is this that darkeneth counsel by words without knowledge?

Gird up now thy loins like a man; for I will demand of thee, and answer thou me.

Where wast thou when I laid the foundations of the earth? declare, if thou hast understanding.

Job 38:1-4

Man that is born of a woman is of few days, and full of trouble.

He cometh forth like a flower, and is cut down: he fleeth also as a shadow, and continueth not.

Job 14:1, 2

Although affliction cometh not forth of the dust, neither doth trouble spring out of the ground;

Yet man is born unto trouble, as the sparks fly upward.

Job 5:6, 7

Like as a father pitieth his children, so the LORD pitieth them that fear him.

For he knoweth our frame; he remembereth that we are dust.

As for man, his days are as grass: as a flower of the field, so he flourisheth.

For the wind passeth over it, and it is gone; and the place thereof shall know it no more.

But the mercy of the LORD is from everlasting to everlasting upon them that fear him, and his righteousness unto children's children;

Psalms 103:13-17

God Works Through You

Humble yourselves therefore under the mighty hand of God, that he may exalt you in due time:

I Peter 5:6

Then said I, Ah, Lord GOD! behold, I cannot speak: for I am a child.

But the LORD said unto me, Say not, I am a child: for thou shalt go to all that I shall send thee, and whatsoever I command thee thou shalt speak.

Be not afraid of their faces: for I am with thee to deliver thee, saith the LORD.

Then the LORD put forth his hand, and touched my mouth. And the LORD said unto me, Behold, I have put my words in thy mouth.

Jeremiah 1:6-9

What is man, that thou art mindful of him? and the son of man, that thou visitest him?

For thou hast made him a little lower than the angels, and hast crowned him with glory and honour.

Thou madest him to have dominion over the works of thy hands; thou hast put all things under his feet:

All sheep and oxen, yea, and the beasts of the field;

The fowl of the air, and the fish of the sea, and whatsoever passeth through the paths of the seas.

O LORD our Lord, how excellent is thy name in all the earth!

Psalms 8:4-9

Some trust in chariots, and some in horses: but we will remember the name of the LORD our God.

They are brought down and fallen: but we are risen, and stand upright.

Psalms 20:7, 8

For then shalt thou have thy delight in the Almighty, and shalt lift up thy face unto God.

Thou shalt make thy prayer unto him, and he shall hear thee, and thou shalt pay thy vows.

Thou shalt also decree a thing, and it shall be established unto thee: and the light shall shine upon thy ways.

When men are cast down, then thou shalt say, There is lifting up; and he shall save the humble person.

Job 22:26-29

O Lord, open thou my lips; and my mouth shall shew forth thy praise.

For thou desirest not sacrifice; else would I give it: thou delightest not in burnt offering.

The sacrifices of God are a broken spirit: a broken and a contrite heart, O God, thou wilt not despise.

Do good in thy good pleasure unto Zion: build thou the walls of Jerusalem.

Psalms 51:15-18

Then shall ye call upon me, and ye shall go and pray unto me, and I will hearken unto you.

And ye shall seek me, and find me, when ye shall search for me with all your heart.

Jeremiah 29:12, 13

When You Feel Life Should Be Easy But Your Spouse Is An Invalid...

God Offers You His Strength

In the day when I cried thou answeredst me, and strengthenedst me with strength in my soul.

Psalms 138:3

I had fainted, unless I had believed to see the goodness of the LORD in the land of the living.

Wait on the LORD: be of good courage, and he shall strengthen thine heart: wait, I say, on the LORD.

Psalms 27:13, 14

Cast thy burden upon the LORD, and he shall sustain thee: he shall never suffer the righteous to be moved.

Psalms 55:22

My flesh and my heart faileth: but God is the strength of my heart, and my portion for ever.

Psalms 73:26

The LORD is my strength and my shield; my heart trusted in him, and I am helped: therefore my heart greatly rejoiceth; and with my song will I praise him.

The LORD is their strength, and he is the saving strength of his anointed.

Save thy people, and bless thine inheritance: feed them also, and lift them up for ever.

Psalms 28:7-9

For I the LORD thy God will hold thy right hand, saying unto thee, Fear not; I will help thee.

Isaiah 41:13

The LORD is good, a strong hold in the day of trouble; and he knoweth them that trust in him.

Nahum 1:7

WHEN YOU FEEL LIFE SHOULD BE EASY BUT YOUR SPOUSE IS AN INVALID

God Gives You His Patience

Cast not away therefore your confidence, which hath great recompence of reward.

For ye have need of patience, that, after ye have done the will of God, ye might receive the promise.

Hebrews 10:35, 36

We are bound to thank God always for you, brethren, as it is meet, because that your faith groweth exceedingly, and the charity of every one of you all toward each other aboundeth;

So that we ourselves glory in you in the churches of God for your patience and faith in all your persecutions and tribulations that ye endure:

II Thessalonians 1:3, 4

He that is slow to anger is better than the mighty; and he that ruleth his spirit than he that taketh a city.

Proverbs 16:32

Take, my brethren, the prophets, who have spoken in the name of the Lord, for an example of suffering affliction, and of patience.

Behold, we count them happy which endure. Ye have heard of the patience of Job, and have seen the end of the Lord; that the Lord is very pitiful, and of tender mercy.

James 5:10, 11

Wherefore seeing we also are compassed about with so great a cloud of witnesses, let us lay aside every weight, and the sin which doth so easily beset us, and let us run with patience the race that is set before us,

Hebrews 12:1

And beside this, giving all diligence, add to your faith virtue; and to virtue knowledge;

And to knowledge temperance; and to temperance patience; and to patience godliness;

And to godliness brotherly kindness; and to brotherly kindness charity.

For if these things be in you, and abound, they make you that ye shall neither be barren nor unfruitful in the knowledge of our Lord Jesus Christ.

II Peter 1:5-8

WHEN YOU FEEL LIFE SHOULD BE EASY BUT YOUR SPOUSE IS AN INVALID

God Tells You How To Live When Life Is Tough

A merry heart doeth good like a medicine: but a broken spirit drieth the bones.

Proverbs 17:22

Heaviness in the heart of man maketh it stoop: but a good word maketh it glad.

Proverbs 12:25

A soft answer turneth away wrath: but grievous words stir up anger.

Proverbs 15:1

Therefore if thou bring thy gift to the altar, and there rememberest that thy brother hath ought against thee;

Leave there thy gift before the altar, and go thy way; first be reconciled to thy brother, and then come and offer thy gift.

Matthew 5:23, 24

If there be therefore any consolation in Christ, if any comfort of love, if any fellowship of the Spirit, if any bowels and mercies,

Fulfil ye my joy, that ye be likeminded, having the same love, being of one accord, of one mind.

Let nothing be done through strife or vainglory; but in lowliness of mind let each esteem other better than themselves.

Philippians 2:1-3

We then that are strong ought to bear the infirmities of the weak, and not to please ourselves.

Romans 15:1

I therefore, the prisoner of the Lord, beseech you that ye walk worthy of the vocation wherewith ye are called,

With all lowliness and meekness, with longsuffering, forbearing one another in love;

Endeavouring to keep the unity of the Spirit in the bond of peace.

There is one body, and one Spirit, even as ye are called in one hope of your calling;

One Lord, one faith, one baptism,

One God and Father of all, who is above all, and through all, and in you all.

But unto every one of us is given grace according to the measure of the gift of Christ.

Ephesians 4:1-7

When You Feel Life Should Be Easy But Your Parents Need Your Help...

God Gives You Direction

Children, obey your parents in all things: for this is well pleasing unto the Lord.

Colossians 3:20

A wise son maketh a glad father: but a foolish man despiseth his mother.

Proverbs 15:20

And he said unto them, Full well ye reject the commandment of God, that ye may keep your own tradition.

For Moses said, Honour thy father and thy mother; and, Whoso curseth father or mother, let him die the death:

But ye say, If a man shall say to his father or mother, It is Corban, that is to say, a gift, by whatsoever thou mightest be profited by me; he shall be free.

And ye suffer him no more to do ought for his father or his mother;

Making the word of God of none effect through your tradition, which ye have delivered: and many such like things do ye.

Mark 7:9-13

Whoso robbeth his father or his mother, and saith, It is no transgression; the same is the companion of a destroyer.

Proverbs 28:24

Honour widows that are widows indeed.

But if any widow have children or nephews, let them learn first to shew piety at home, and to requite their parents: for that is good and acceptable before God.

I Timothy 5:3, 4

Sanctify yourselves therefore, and be ye holy: for I am the LORD your God.

And ye shall keep my statutes, and do them: I am the LORD which sanctify you.

For every one that curseth his father or his mother shall be surely put to death: he hath cursed his father or his mother; his blood shall be upon him.

Leviticus 20:7-9

God Adds A Blessing

Children, obey your parents in the Lord: for this is right.

Honour thy father and mother; which is the first commandment with promise;

That it may be well with thee, and thou mayest live long on the earth.

Ephesians 6:1-3

And if thou wilt walk in my ways, to keep my statutes and my commandments, as thy father David did walk, then I will lengthen thy days.

I Kings 3:14

Now the days of David drew nigh that he should die; and he charged Solomon his son, saying,

I go the way of all the earth: be thou strong therefore, and shew thyself a man;

And keep the charge of the LORD thy God, to walk in his ways, to keep his statutes, and his commandments, and his judgments, and his testimonies, as it is written in the law of Moses, that thou mayest prosper in all that thou doest, and whithersoever thou turnest thyself:

I Kings 2:1-3

Honour thy father and thy mother: that thy days may be long upon the land which the LORD thy God giveth thee.

Exodus 20:12

WHEN YOU FEEL LIFE SHOULD BE EASY BUT YOUR PARENTS NEED YOUR HELP

God Reminds You He Is Your Father Too

And it came to pass, that, as he was praying in a certain place, when he ceased, one of his disciples said unto him, Lord, teach us to pray, as John also taught his disciples.

And he said unto them, When ye pray, say, Our Father which art in heaven, Hallowed be thy name. Thy kingdom come. Thy will be done, as in heaven, so in earth.

Luke 11:1, 2

But now, O LORD, thou art our father; we are the clay, and thou our potter; and we all are the work of thy hand.

Isaiah 64:8

Let your light so shine before men, that they may see your good works, and glorify your Father which is in heaven.

Matthew 5:16

Do ye thus requite the LORD, O foolish people and unwise? is not he thy father that hath bought thee? hath he not made thee, and established thee?

Deuteronomy 32:6

Be ye therefore followers of God, as dear children;

Ephesians 5:1

Behold, what manner of love the Father hath bestowed upon us, that we should be called the sons of God: therefore the world knoweth us not, because it knew him not.

I John 3:1

When You Feel Life Should Be Easy But Your Children Are Far From God…

God Gives You Hope

Put not your trust in princes, nor in the son of man, in whom there is no help.

His breath goeth forth, he returneth to his earth; in that very day his thoughts perish.

Happy is he that hath the God of Jacob for his help, whose hope is in the LORD his God:

Psalms 146:3-5

Be of good courage, and he shall strengthen your heart, all ye that hope in the LORD.

Psalms 31:24

And now, Lord, what wait I for? my hope is in thee.

Psalms 39:7

Why art thou cast down, O my soul? and why art thou disquieted in me? hope thou in God: for I shall yet praise him for the help of his countenance.

Psalms 42:5

But I will hope continually, and will yet praise thee more and more.

Psalms 71:14

Blessed is the man that trusteth in the LORD, and whose hope the LORD is.

Jeremiah 17:7

WHEN YOU FEEL LIFE SHOULD BE EASY BUT YOUR CHILDREN ARE FAR FROM GOD

God Shares Your Concern

The LORD upholdeth all that fall, and raiseth up all those that be bowed down.

The eyes of all wait upon thee; and thou givest them their meat in due season.

Thou openest thine hand, and satisfiest the desire of every living thing.

The LORD is righteous in all his ways, and holy in all his works.

The LORD is nigh unto all them that call upon him, to all that call upon him in truth.

He will fulfil the desire of them that fear him: he also will hear their cry, and will save them.

Psalms 145:14-19

Cause me to hear thy lovingkindness in the morning; for in thee do I trust: cause me to know the way wherein I should walk; for I lift up my soul unto thee.

Psalms 143:8

The LORD is far from the wicked: but he heareth the prayer of the righteous.

Proverbs 15:29

The spirit of the Lord GOD is upon me; because the LORD hath anointed me to preach good tidings unto the meek; he hath sent me to bind up the brokenhearted, to proclaim liberty to the captives, and the opening of the prison to them that are bound;

To proclaim the acceptable year of the LORD, and the day of vengeance of our God; to comfort all that mourn;

Isaiah 61:1, 2

For we are saved by hope: but hope that is seen is not hope: for what a man seeth, why doth he yet hope for?

But if we hope for that we see not, then do we with patience wait for it.

Likewise the Spirit also helpeth our infirmities: for we know not what we should pray for as we ought: but the Spirit itself maketh intercession for us with groanings which cannot be uttered.

And he that searcheth the hearts knoweth what is the mind of the Spirit, because he maketh intercession for the saints according to the will of God.

And we know that all things work together for good to them that love God, to them who are the called according to his purpose.

Romans 8:24-28

And he is before all things, and by him all things consist.

And he is the head of the body, the church: who is the beginning, the firstborn from the dead; that in all things he might have the preeminence.

For it pleased the Father that in him should all fulness dwell;

And, having made peace through the blood of his cross, by him to reconcile all things unto himself; by him, I say, whether they be things in earth, or things in heaven.

Colossians 1:17-20

God Assures You Of His Love For Them

For the Son of man is come to save that which was lost.

How think ye? if a man have an hundred sheep, and one of them be gone astray, doth he not leave the ninety and nine, and goeth into the mountains, and seeketh that which is gone astray?

And if so be that he find it, verily I say unto you, he rejoiceth more of that sheep, than of the ninety and nine which went not astray.

Even so it is not the will of your Father which is in heaven, that one of these little ones should perish.

Matthew 18:11-14

But Jesus called them unto him, and said, Suffer little children to come unto me, and forbid them not: for of such is the kingdom of God.

Luke 18:16

If ye then, being evil, know how to give good gifts unto your children: how much more shall your heavenly Father give the Holy Spirit to them that ask him?

Luke 11:13

For the unbelieving husband is sanctified by the wife, and the unbelieving wife is sanctified by the husband: else were your children unclean; but now are they holy.

I Corinthians 7:14

Train up a child in the way he should go: and when he is old, he will not depart from it.

Proverbs 22:6

My mercy will I keep for him for evermore, and my covenant shall stand fast with him.

His seed also will I make to endure for ever, and his throne as the days of heaven.

If his children forsake my law, and walk not in my judgments;

If they break my statutes, and keep not my commandments;

Then will I visit their transgression with the rod, and their iniquity with stripes.

Nevertheless my lovingkindness will I not utterly take from him, nor suffer my faithfulness to fail.

Psalms 89:28-33

When You Add Up Life's Score And Have Run A Good Race...

God Promises You A Great Reward

Blessed are ye, when men shall revile you, and persecute you, and shall say all manner of evil against you falsely, for my sake.

Rejoice, and be exceeding glad: for great is your reward in heaven: for so persecuted they the prophets which were before you.

Matthew 5:11, 12

So that a man shall say, Verily there is a reward for the righteous: verily he is a God that judgeth in the earth.

Psalms 58:11

As righteousness tendeth to life: so he that pursueth evil pursueth it to his own death.

Proverbs 11:19

For other foundation can no man lay than that is laid, which is Jesus Christ.

Now if any man build upon this foundation gold, silver, precious stones, wood, hay, stubble;

Every man's work shall be made manifest: for the day shall declare it, because it shall be revealed by fire; and the fire shall try every man's work of what sort it is.

If any man's work abide which he hath built thereupon, he shall receive a reward.

If any man's work shall be burned, he shall suffer loss: but he himself shall be saved; yet so as by fire.

I Corinthians 3:11-15

But love ye your enemies, and do good, and lend, hoping for nothing again; and your reward shall be great, and ye shall be the children of the Highest: for he is kind unto the unthankful and to the evil.

Luke 6:35

And he lifted up his eyes on his disciples, and said, Blessed be ye poor: for yours is the kingdom of God.

Blessed are ye that hunger now: for ye shall be filled. Blessed are ye that weep now: for ye shall laugh.

Blessed are ye, when men shall hate you, and when they shall separate you from their company, and shall reproach you, and cast out your name as evil, for the Son of man's sake.

Rejoice ye in that day, and leap for joy: for, behold, your reward is great in heaven: for in the like manner did their fathers unto the prophets.

Luke 6:20-23

God Uses Your Good And Faithful Works

Ye are the light of the world. A city that is set on an hill cannot be hid.

Neither do men light a candle, and put it under a bushel, but on a candlestick; and it giveth light unto all that are in the house.

Let your light so shine before men, that they may see your good works, and glorify your Father which is in heaven.

Matthew 5:14-16

The preparations of the heart in man, and the answer of the tongue, is from the LORD.

All the ways of a man are clean in his own eyes; but the LORD weigheth the spirits.

Commit thy works unto the LORD, and thy thoughts shall be established.

Proverbs 16:1-3

Labour not for the meat which perisheth, but for that meat which endureth unto everlasting life, which the Son of man shall give unto you: for him hath God the Father sealed.

Then said they unto him, What shall we do, that we might work the works of God?

Jesus answered and said unto them, This is the work of God, that ye believe on him whom he hath sent.

John 6:27-29

And God is able to make all grace abound toward you; that ye, always having all sufficiency in all things, may abound to every good work:

II Corinthians 9:8

What doth it profit, my brethren, though a man say he hath faith, and have not works? can faith save him?

If a brother or sister be naked, and destitute of daily food,

And one of you say unto them, Depart in peace, be ye warmed and filled; notwithstanding ye give them not those things which are needful to the body; what doth it profit?

Even so faith, if it hath not works, is dead, being alone.

Yea, a man may say, Thou hast faith, and I have works: shew me thy faith without thy works, and I will shew thee my faith by my works.

Thou believest that there is one God; thou doest well: the devils also believe, and tremble.

But wilt thou know, O vain man, that faith without works is dead?

James 2:14-20

WHEN YOU ADD UP LIFE'S SCORE AND HAVE RUN A GOOD RACE

God Asks You To Help Others Do The Same

I press toward the mark for the prize of the high calling of God in Christ Jesus.

Let us therefore, as many as be perfect, be thus minded: and if in any thing ye be otherwise minded, God shall reveal even this unto you.

Nevertheless, whereto we have already attained, let us walk by the same rule, let us mind the same thing.

Brethren, be followers together of me, and mark them which walk so as ye have us for an ensample.

Philippians 3:14-17

I therefore, the prisoner of the Lord, beseech you that ye walk worthy of the vocation wherewith ye are called,

With all lowliness and meekness, with longsuffering, forbearing one another in love;

Endeavouring to keep the unity of the Spirit in the bond of peace.

Ephesians 4:1-3

Brethren, if a man be overtaken in a fault, ye which are spiritual, restore such an one in the spirit of meekness; considering thyself, lest thou also be tempted.

Bear ye one another's burdens, and so fulfil the law of Christ.

For he that soweth to his flesh shall of the flesh reap corruption; but he that soweth to the Spirit shall of the Spirit reap life everlasting.

And let us not be weary in well doing: for in due season we shall reap, if we faint not.

As we have therefore opportunity, let us do good unto all men, especially unto them who are of the household of faith.

Galatians 6:1, 2, 8-10

But none of these things move me, neither count I my life dear unto myself, so that I might finish my course with joy, and the ministry, which I have received of the Lord Jesus, to testify the gospel of the grace of God.

And now, behold, I know that ye all, among whom I have gone preaching the kingdom of God, shall see my face no more.

Wherefore I take you to record this day, that I am pure from the blood of all men.

For I have not shunned to declare unto you all the counsel of God.

Take heed therefore unto yourselves, and to all the flock, over the which the Holy Ghost hath made you overseers, to feed the church of God, which he hath purchased with his own blood.

Acts 20:24-28

Let the word of Christ dwell in you richly in all wisdom; teaching and admonishing one another in psalms and hymns and spiritual songs, singing with grace in your hearts to the Lord.

Colossians 3:16

When You Add Up Life's Score And Realize You Need Help. . .

God Has Mercy On You

Praise ye the LORD. O give thanks unto the LORD; for he is good: for his mercy endureth for ever.

Psalms 106:1

The LORD is merciful and gracious, slow to anger, and plenteous in mercy.

He will not always chide: neither will he keep his anger for ever.

He hath not dealt with us after our sins; nor rewarded us according to our iniquities.

For as the heaven is high above the earth, so great is his mercy toward them that fear him.

Psalms 103:8-11

I will praise thee, O LORD, among the people: and I will sing praises unto thee among the nations.

For thy mercy is great above the heavens: and thy truth reacheth unto the clouds.

Psalms 108:3, 4

The earth, O LORD, is full of thy mercy: teach me thy statutes.

Psalms 119:64

The LORD is gracious, and full of compassion; slow to anger, and of great mercy.

The LORD is good to all: and his tender mercies are over all his works.

Psalms 145:8, 9

But God, who is rich in mercy, for his great love wherewith he loved us,

Even when we were dead in sins, hath quickened us together with Christ, (by grace ye are saved;)

Ephesians 2:4, 5

WHEN YOU ADD UP LIFE'S SCORE AND REALIZE YOU NEED HELP

God Offers You Salvation

Blessed be the Lord, who daily loadeth us with benefits, even the God of our salvation. Selah.

Psalms 68:19

Lead me in thy truth, and teach me: for thou art the God of my salvation; on thee do I wait all the day.

Psalms 25:5

Let all those that seek thee rejoice and be glad in thee: and let such as love thy salvation say continually, Let God be magnified.

Psalms 70:4

Behold, God is my salvation; I will trust, and not be afraid: for the LORD JEHOVAH is my strength and my song; he also is become my salvation.

Isaiah 12:2

For I am not ashamed of the gospel of Christ: for it is the power of God unto salvation to every one that believeth; to the Jew first, and also to the Greek.

Romans 1:16

But we are bound to give thanks alway to God for you, brethren beloved of the Lord, because God hath from the beginning chosen you to salvation through sanctification of the Spirit and belief of the truth:

II Thessalonians 2:13

God Asks Others To Comfort You Also

Wherefore comfort yourselves together, and edify one another, even as also ye do.

I Thessalonians 5:11

And Jacob rent his clothes, and put sackcloth upon his loins, and mourned for his son many days.

And all his sons and all his daughters rose up to comfort him; but he refused to be comforted; and he said, For I will go down into the grave unto my son mourning. Thus his father wept for him.

Genesis 37:34, 35

Now when Job's three friends heard of all this evil that was come upon him, they came every one from his own place; Eliphaz the Temanite, and Bildad the Shuhite, and Zophar the Naamathite: for they had made an appointment together to come to mourn with him and to comfort him.

And when they lifted up their eyes afar off, and knew him not, they lifted up their voice, and wept; and they rent every one his mantle, and sprinkled dust upon their heads toward heaven.

So they sat down with him upon the ground seven days and seven nights, and none spake a word unto him: for they saw that his grief was very great.

Job 2:11-13

And many of the Jews came to Martha and Mary, to comfort them concerning their brother.

John 11:19

We give thanks to God always for you all, making mention of you in our prayers;

Remembering without ceasing your work of faith, and labour of love, and patience of hope in our Lord Jesus Christ, in the sight of God and our Father;

Knowing, brethren beloved, your election of God.

I Thessalonians 1:2-4

For the Lord himself shall descend from heaven with a shout, with the voice of the archangel, and with the trump of God: and the dead in Christ shall rise first:

Then we which are alive and remain shall be caught up together with them in the clouds, to meet the Lord in the air: and so shall we ever be with the Lord.

Wherefore comfort one another with these words.

I Thessalonians 4:16-18

PERSONAL STUDY NOTES

PERSONAL STUDY NOTES

love you Mom 12/95